Collegeville Ministry Series

THE MINISTRY OF THE ASSEMBLY

Joyce Ann Zimmerman, CPPS

LITURGICAL PRESS

Collegeville, Minnesota

www.litpress.org

Excerpts from documents of the Second Vatican Council are from *Vatican Council II: Constitutions, Decrees, Declarations; The Basic Sixteen Documents*, edited by Austin Flannery, OP, © 1996. Used with permission of Liturgical Press, Collegeville, Minnesota.

Scripture texts in this work are taken from the *New Revised Standard Version Bible: Catholic Edition* © 1989, 1993, Division of Christian Education of the National Council of the Churches of Christ in the United States of America. Used by permission. All rights reserved.

Excerpts from the English translation of *The Roman Missal, Third Edition* © 2010, International Commission on English in the Liturgy Corporation (ICEL). Excerpts from the English translation of General Instruction of the Roman Missal © 2007, ICEL. All rights reserved.

© 2016 by Order of Saint Benedict, Collegeville, Minnesota. All rights reserved. No part of this book may be reproduced in any form, by print, microfilm, microfiche, mechanical recording, photocopying, translation, or by any other means, known or yet unknown, for any purpose except brief quotations in reviews, without the previous written permission of Liturgical Press, Saint John's Abbey, PO Box 7500, Collegeville, Minnesota 56321-7500. Printed in the United States of America.

1	2	3	4	5	6	7	8	9

Library of Congress Control Number: 2015947056

ISBN: 978-0-8146-4856-8   978-0-8146-4881-0 (ebook)

Contents

Introduction   1

1 The *Being* of the Liturgical Assembly   9

2 The *Doing* of the Liturgical Assembly   19

3 The *Why* of the Liturgical Assembly   32

4 The *Place* of the Liturgical Assembly   38

5 A *Spirituality* of the Liturgical Assembly   47

Conclusion   68

Notes   71

Introduction

We all know who a couch potato is—one who sits for hours on end mindlessly watching TV. We all know who a bump on a log is—one who is stuck, can't get going, inert. We all know who a spectator sports person is—one who watches rather than participates in an activity. What all these folks have in common is lack of energy, ambition, enthusiasm, participation, accomplishment. They are largely disengaged and seem happy to be passive.

The liturgical assembly has nothing in common with couch potatoes, bumps on a log, or spectator sports persons. The liturgical assembly—those gathered for liturgy—is made up of vital participants in a vital activity. Each assembly member has her or his own role to play: "*All*, therefore, whether ordained ministers or lay Christian faithful, in fulfilling their function or their duty, should *carry out* solely but *totally* that which pertains to them."[1] No one ought to come to liturgy just to be there.

Liturgy is a celebration of God's saving deeds involving a lively divine-human exchange—an encounter with dialogue between the assembly and God, the assembly and presider, the assembly and each other. This dialogue is far more than words. Liturgy's divine-human exchange is a communion of mind and hearts, a grace-laden Self-giving and self-giving, a surrender of self to be more than we are.

Our language can belie appropriate attitudes for an understanding of liturgy. We say we are "going to church" or "attending Mass." Probably most people simply do not think about the meaning of such phrases. These phrases imply that we consider liturgy as something "out there," not part of us, external to who we are. Not so! Not to surrender self to the assembly is to keep us apart from entering into why we are baptized and why we choose to live a Christian life. Liturgy, as we shall see throughout this book, celebrates who we are and who we are becoming.

Overlooked Ministry

When we hear the word "ministry," we might think first of priests, ordained ministers. Since Vatican II, we have come to appreciate lay involvement in what we might call "visible" liturgical ministries. Most of our parishes have scores of people who serve as lectors, extraordinary ministers of Holy Communion, altar servers (or acolytes), musicians, choir members, cantors, hospitality ministers (or ushers and greeters), sacristans, environment ministers, deacons. These ministers are directly connected with the unfolding of the liturgy proper. Additionally, we might have leaders of the Liturgy of the Word for children, leaders who break open the Scriptures with catechumens, supervisors in a children's nursery, coordinators of liturgy, and coordinators of seasonal changes in the environment.

As many as these people are, there are many other people who come to Sunday Mass or other liturgical celebrations who are not one of these visible ministers responsible for the unfolding of the actual liturgy. If we ask them what their ministry is during Mass, they might give us a blank stare. This book is about helping *everyone* at liturgy understand that *being there* is a ministry, that is, the ministry of the assembly. In fact, in some respects the ministry of the assembly is the most important ministry of all.

Our gathering in the church for liturgy is far more than simply getting our bodies there. The liturgical assembly makes visible the church, the Body of Christ, by its very gathering together as one Body. As *liturgical* assembly it makes present the celebration of the paschal mystery and Christ's ongoing mystery of salvation. The ministry of the assembly is first and foremost to *be* the Body of Christ, surrendering to Christ's presence, and being transformed into ever-more perfect members of his Body. When we gather as liturgical assembly, we fulfill our baptismal identity as graced daughters and sons of God. When we gather as liturgical assembly, we call to mind and live out our identity as Christians to be the church, the Body of Christ. We are church made visible. We are the members of Christ's Body now gathered around Christ, the Head of his Body.

What we *do* is important: we sit, stand, and kneel; we sing and pray; we give and receive; we interact with others and encounter God. All this doing, however, is empty—is going through mere motions—if we are not also *being*. Our *being* the assembly requires other-centeredness, surrendering to God's transforming action during Mass, accepting diversity, recognizing each member's place and role in this diversity, focusing on our common identity under Jesus Christ, committing ourselves to celebrating Mass wholeheartedly, hearing the dismissal at the end of Mass as a command from Christ to live what we have celebrated. Understanding ourselves in this light is what this book is all about.

Ministry as Being and Doing

The various liturgical ministries are, to some extent, about getting a "job" done. The readings need to be proclaimed, the gifts and altar need to be prepared, prayers need to be prayed, Christ's Body and Blood need to be distributed. Each minister, in fact, has a "job" to do. But if that were all there is to it, there might be better ways to go about ministering than forming and scheduling people, which, we all admit, can sometimes be a time-consuming effort. To move from getting a job done to truly being a minister means that underlying the *doing* must be a *being*. In other words, each ministry has a spirituality (a way of living) in which it is grounded. When the minister lives the particular spirituality, he or she is truly *being* the ministry; if not, he or she is simply getting a job done.

Being the ministry comes first. What we mean by this is that we must live our baptismal identity—to be the Body of Christ—from the perspective of the particular ministry we have embraced. Basic to this kind of living is the rhythm of the paschal mystery. While preparing to minister and while ministering during Mass or other liturgical occasions, we are visible icons of Christ's death and resurrection, of his self-emptying and exaltation, of his poverty of self and fullness of risen life. Embodying this rhythm in our daily living and celebration of liturgy immerses us in the mission of Christ, is essential to our identity as members of the Body of Christ, and informs all we do. *Being* the ministry means we live it before we come to the celebration of Mass. So our doing at liturgy flows from our being a minister who lives the particular ministry every day.

At the same time, *doing* the ministry is surely not unimportant. No matter what our particular ministry, we participate in all of liturgy (not just while we are doing our ministry) in such a way that we *model* the rhythm of the paschal mystery from our lived experience of it. Further, *doing* our ministry is a concrete way to share with our sisters and brothers in Christ the unique gift given us by the Holy Spirit at baptism to build up the Body of Christ.

Always, both the *being* and *doing* of our ministry brings us to Christ. It is Christ's mystery we celebrate at liturgy; it is Christ who is present in continual self-giving; it is Christ who is present within us and to us who leads us ever-deeper into the mystery of salvation. The being and doing of the assembly is explored more extensively in the first two chapters of this book.

Why We Assemble

If we ask people gathering for liturgy why they are there, we might be surprised at the wide variety of answers we receive. Some come because it is expected of them; some because that's simply what they do on Sunday; some because it's an obligation; some because they meet family and friends there; some because they want to pray; some because they . . . and on and on. Actually, all of these responses have some value to them. As we learn more and more about what liturgy is, however, we come to understand how much more is happening at liturgy than we can externally observe or express in words.

Liturgy transforms us into being more perfect members of the Body of Christ into which we were baptized. This unique and holy identity means that we are to be the presence of the risen Christ in the world in which we live. We encounter Jesus' ceaseless self-giving at liturgy, and are strengthened to be that self-giving for those we meet in our daily living. Liturgy helps us connect God, self, and world. These connections are grasped through the ritual actions and symbols, through the assembly's gestures and postures, through prayer and reverence. All of this is the focus of the next two chapters on the why and place of the liturgical assembly.

Living the Liturgy

In the past we have tended to limit our understanding of the sacraments in terms of actions that bestow graces. While that is certainly true, since the liturgical renewal after the Second Vatican Council we have come to understand the fruit of the sacraments in a much broader and more demanding way. Grace is God's life, a theological term we might use to describe our relationship with God. But this relationship is not simply "vertical"—God and me. My relationship with God spills over into how I relate to my family and friends, coworkers and casual acquaintances. My relationship with God spills over into how I live. Living the liturgy is a spirituality, the church's spirituality, a spirituality grounded in the paschal mystery. The assembly's liturgical spirituality is the discussion of the last chapter, which brings us, in another way, to how the fruits of the liturgical action don't stay within the walls of the church building but spill out into our everyday living. Liturgy is for living.

Why This Book?

The Ministry of the Assembly is a new book in Liturgical Press's ministry series. The other books are directed to the "visible," individual ministries that enable liturgy to unfold with dignity and grace, beauty and reverence. Certainly, these ministers and ministries are important, as we've already said; liturgy cannot happen without them. Affirming this, however, does not relegate the ministry of the assembly to something secondary; the ministry of every single person gathered is essential. The visible liturgical ministers are there to serve the liturgy, which is also to say, to serve the assembly.

This book is obviously directed to everyone "in the pews," everyone who embraces the ministry of the assembly. A more focused target group of readers would be those engaged in the RCIA process; this book would help them understand who they are and how liturgy continues to form them in their baptismal identity and mission. This book would help the baptized and catechumens alike understand with more depth who they are as church and how liturgy commits us over and over again to Gospel living.

One of the desires of the Vatican II council fathers was education for the liturgy, not only for priests and seminarians, but for all the faithful: "With diligence and patience pastors of souls should see to the liturgical instruction of the faithful. . . . "[2] To this end, the chapters include descriptions of the liturgical centers and sacred spaces, objects and symbols used in the liturgy, gestures and postures of the assembly, seasons and festivals, various elements of liturgy. Pulled out of the chapters and put together, these brief descriptions are a kind of "liturgical dictionary" that afford opportunities to grow in our liturgical vocabulary and understanding and would help new Catholics or prospective Catholics to become familiar with Catholic vocabulary and traditions. For the sake of clarity and brevity, most of our discussion focuses on the eucharistic liturgy, the Mass. Mass is our weekly celebration of who we are and are becoming in Christ. Our reflections, however, would largely apply to other liturgies as well—the celebration of the other six sacraments and the Liturgy of the Hours. The assembly also has a ministry at these other celebrations, and this ought not to be forgotten.

Being a liturgical assembly is a privilege of our baptismal identity. Because being a liturgical assembly is a visible expression of who we are, we want to prepare, celebrate, and live liturgy as best as we can. We can never take liturgy for granted. To use the words of the council fathers, the liturgy "is supremely effective in enabling the faithful to express in their lives and portray to others the mystery of Christ and the real nature of the true church" (SC 2).

1

The *Being* of
the Liturgical Assembly

The word "assembly" obviously implies a group of people who have come together for a common purpose. Some legislative bodies are called assemblies, for example, the General Assembly of the United Nations. While this very broad definition of assembly is applicable to the liturgical assembly, there is much more at stake. The word "liturgical" modifying "assembly" makes all the difference in the world. This isn't any assembling of people; the liturgical assembly is a gathering of the baptized to be before their God in worship.

The Hebrew word for a gathering of people is *qahal*. It is a word that is used when Israel is an assembly before God, that is, when Israel is a worshiping community, a communion of people called by God. The word "community" itself is revealing. From the Latin words *cum* and *unus*, "one with," the notion of community is more than a conglomerate of people, even if there is a common purpose. The unity of the worshiping assembly before God suggests that there is a shared being, a shared identity. And there is. Baptized in Christ Jesus, we are made members of his one Body. The Christian community is called an "assembly" when we are gathered for liturgy, and in that context we understand ourselves precisely as *being before God*. Moreover, we are not an assembly simply by being together. We are a *liturgical* assembly because God calls us into divine presence. God calls, we respond. Our response is to surrender ourselves to be drawn more deeply into the saving mystery of Christ that is being celebrated.

The liturgical assembly manifests the church, the Body of Christ, in all its fullness. As *liturgical* assembly it is the instrument for making present the paschal mystery and for Christ's ongoing work of salvation. When we gather as liturgical assembly, we call to mind and live out our identity as Christians to be the church, the Body of Christ. These statements become clearer when we consider what, really, happens at our baptism. This first sacrament is not merely a ritual ceremony that happens in a specific place at a specific time. Baptism is an initiation into a way of life to which we continually say yes, continually renew our commitment, continually seek to live more fully.

Call of Baptism

Sometimes we might hear adolescents objecting to their being baptized as infants with something like, "I'm mad because my parents did this to me and now I feel caught; it wasn't my choice." In fact, the statement communicates a sad misunderstanding about baptism (and, indeed, all the sacraments). Baptism is hardly a once-and-for-all event with the infant (or anyone else, for that matter!) being a passive recipient. Baptism is an *initiation* into Christian living. We receive new life in the Spirit, become a child of God and a member of the Body of Christ. This new life *begins* a way of living—a direction for choices—that lasts our whole lifetime. This means that baptism's fruitfulness implies an *ongoing yes* on the part of the one who is baptized. We enter into so great a mystery that we spend our whole lives working out how we respond to it. Essentially, our baptismal response is a constant *yes* to God's will in our lives, a constant ratification of our identity as the Body of Christ, a *growing into* living the dying and rising mystery of Christ and our regeneration as children of God.

With respect to infant baptism, objections concerning the infant's inability to make a commitment miss the point. Other issues around the parents, godparents, and liturgical assembly raise more telling questions about the meaning of baptism—of our identity as Body of Christ, members of the Christian community, and participation in the mission of the church. Instead of a limited focus on original sin and remission of sin, we must move in the direction of a positive, life-giving understanding of this important sacrament. The ritual expression itself carries us beyond ourselves into the realm of the Spirit and shows us how life in the Spirit identifies who we are as baptized Christians.

Many parents (especially mothers) of infants baptized before Vatican II's liturgical revisions were not even present at their newborn children's baptisms. Often it was the sponsors who brought the infant to church and expressed the parents' wish to have the baby baptized. The ceremony was largely a private one, didn't take very long, and happened in a small, out-of-the-way space ("closet") that contained the baptismal font and not much else. No explanation was given for the rites. A little water was sprinkled. And it was over. In this context it is very easy to miss the deepest reality of baptism as being plunged into Christ's death and sharing in his new life of the resurrection.

Our revised rite changes all this. The prayers, symbols, and gestures invite participation by all who are present. We know this liturgy is a *community* experience. The rite demands our full participation. When the symbols and gestures are "maximized"—used to the fullest—the ritual event has the potential to convey a power unequaled by very many human experiences. When the person being baptized is signed not only by the presider but by the family and representative community members, when enough oil is used that the person glistens, when enough water is used to fully immerse, when the person is dried and dressed in white and presented to and received by the whole community, when the baptismal candle is large and presented in such a way as to communicate inherent dignity—then the symbols work to convey the attraction and power of this sacrament. When this is all so, then we have a deeper understanding that baptism isn't something "done to us." Instead, it is a rite celebrating our identity as graced children of God who walk in the light of Christ. Maybe then our *yes* will be even more true and ongoing.

St. Paul asks a very pointed and direct question in his Letter to the Romans, one that we must ask ourselves again and again these two thousand years later: "*Do you not know* that all of us who have been baptized into Christ Jesus were baptized into his death? Therefore we have been buried with him by baptism into death, so that, just as Christ was raised from the dead by the glory of the Father, so we too might walk in newness of life" (Rom 6:3-4; italics added). Actually, we don't know very well. These many years after Vatican II we haven't moved, in the main, beyond understanding baptism primarily as removing sin. A Pauline baptismal theology—the one that has largely formed the Western, Latin Church members—is less concerned with what is "removed" by baptism (the old self with its sinfulness) but is far more concerned with what is gained (a new life in the risen Christ). So many of the symbols associated with baptism, especially the paschal candle and white garment, point to a whole new revelation of God's wondrous acceptance of us and the new life that we live because of that divine election.

A sign of that election is the many gifts that God lavishes on us out of love and fidelity. By ourselves, it is so true, we can never be worthy of these unthinkable riches. But it is God who calls. And in that we are worthy.

Each baptized Christian is given a unique gift—task, ministry—in order to build up the Body of Christ. The references to gifts and ministries scattered throughout the writings of Paul (see especially 1 Cor 12) are particularly helpful for our consideration of baptism and the ministry of the liturgical assembly. Ministry is a consequence of our baptismal call. So is life in the Spirit. So is a unique gift of the Spirit given to each of us. Note, though, that Paul insists the gifts are not given for the sake of the individual, but for the sake of the community. Also, each community has all the gifts that it needs for it to come to full stature in Christ (unless gifts are refused or not exercised for the good of all). Our ministry as an assembly, then, is a ministry to each other. We help each other come before God. We help each other surrender to the mystery being celebrated. We help each other become one in Christ's Body.

Think about it: in baptism the old self dies and we are raised up to share in the risen life of Christ. We are given a new identity: Body of Christ. We become one with Christ. This communion of identity is what is expressed when we assemble for liturgy. It begins with the baptismal ritual and continues throughout our life.

The baptismal font. Originally, baptisms most likely took place in rivers or streams of flowing, living waters. "In those days Jesus came from Nazareth of Galilee and was baptized by John in the Jordan" (Mark 1:9). The event of Philip's encounter with the Ethiopian eunuch recounted in the Acts of the Apostles gives us a similar picture of early baptisms occurring at places where water was abundant: "As they were going along the road, they came to some water; and the eunuch said, 'Look, here is water! What is to prevent me from being baptized?' He commanded the chariot to stop, and both of them, Philip and the eunuch, went down into the water, and Philip baptized him" (Acts 8:36-38). Baptism implies plentiful water, so the sign of being cleansed and receiving new life is aptly clear. An abundance of water carries a very powerful message: often water is life-threatening; people can drown in too much water. In the early church baptismal fonts were large, often in the shape of a sarcophagus, a tomb. The one to be baptized would be led down into the water and, at the trinitarian names, would be plunged under, a poignant gesture of dying to self. After three times being plunged, the newly baptized would be brought up out of the sarcophagus-font and clothed in a white garment, a sign of having risen to new life in Christ. The symbols used were large and hard to miss. The waters of baptism bring both death and life.

The font's placement. One knotty problem in building new liturgical spaces or renovating old ones is the placement of the baptismal font. Many liturgists favor its location at the entrance to the worship space. Here, all can dip their hands in the *flowing* water (like a river or stream; in spite of being called a "font," it is not a "fountain") and bless themselves as a reminder that we enter the sacred space and become visible church, the liturgical assembly, because we have been immersed in those baptismal waters. Logistically, placing the font at the entrance creates at least three challenges. First, most church buildings have more than one entrance; it can be very difficult to change people's patterns and usher them all through a single main entrance. Small holy water fonts can be placed at all the entrances (as has been the custom), but this diminishes the symbolic power of the font itself and many people do not associate these small water receptacles and blessing themselves with water with the baptismal font and their baptism. Second, the shape and size of some buildings can prevent people from seeing the ritual action at a font placed at the entrance; sound alone is not enough for full participation (this also implies that the gathering space must be large enough to hold the assembly). Third, many communities have addressed these problems by having a large, permanent font at the entrance and then a smaller, "portable" font for other occasions (e.g., baptism of infants during a Sunday liturgy or baptisms at the Easter Vigil). Multiple fonts compromise the symbolism of the one font, one baptism we all share.

Immersion. Much talk takes place these days about baptism by immersion. This more easily happens with infants where the font doesn't have to be very large in order to completely immerse the infant. Many of our renovations have included baptismal fonts that are at least two or three feet deep into which the presider and older children or adults can enter. A great deal of water is poured over the individual being baptized, and this is surely a symbolic improvement over a little bit of water being poured on a head held over a small font (which form is still permitted). Nonetheless, it is good to remind ourselves that while immersion is an improvement over using only a little bit of water, immersion still isn't *submersion*, as happened in the early church. Baptism by submersion implies that the *whole body* is plunged into the water; this most clearly symbolizes *death* to the old self. How practical is this? Not very! But at least let us use enough water during baptism to carry its double meaning of death and life.

Summons of God

Parents call their children to dinner. Teachers call their class to order. Bosses call staff meetings to convene. When we are summoned to something, however, we note an urgency, a "can't not respond" situation, a command performance at something that is important. Courts might send out a summons that is an order to appear rather than an invitation to come or not. To ignore a court summons means contempt of court that can result in a pretty stiff fine.

We think of God nowadays as good and gracious and gentle. So, to speak of a summons by God might at first glance seem rather harsh and out of character for God. Our gracious God usually calls us—gently invites us and we have the free will to accept or not. On occasion, however, God summons us, and this we cannot ignore.

Church law still stipulates that we have an obligation to be at Mass on Sundays. Saturday evening Masses are not "anticipated" Masses of Sunday, but are truly Sunday Mass because on all Sundays and high feast days we reckon a day not from midnight to midnight like we usually do, but from sundown to sundown. We might consider this obligation to be at Sunday Mass to be a "summons" from God, and one that we cannot ignore.

Before he ascended into heaven, Jesus gave his disciples what we call the "great commission": "Go therefore and make disciples of all nations, baptizing them in the name of the Father and of the Son and of the Holy Spirit, and teaching them to obey everything that I have commanded you" (Matt 28:19-20). In Luke's account of the Last Supper, Jesus tells his disciples that they are to "[d]o this in remembrance of me" (Luke 22:19). After Jesus had washed the disciples' feet in John's Last Supper account, he says to them, "For I have set you an example, that you also should do as I have done to you" (13:15). In all these instances, and countless others in the gospels, Jesus is not simply inviting. He is commanding, he is summoning his followers to some particular action.

Some things about our Christian faith are so fundamental that they really leave no choice but to answer the summons. Our coming together as a liturgical assembly is an answer to Jesus' summons to carry forth his saving ministry. We are not simply at liturgy for ourselves. We are there to make present and visible his saving actions. We are there to surrender being individual members of the Body of Christ to being the Body of Christ united with Christ the Head; in this act of surrender we are church made visible. There is no greater summons. There is no greater response than to say yes to who we are and who we are becoming. In our response, together as a liturgical assembly we mediate God's saving grace. Mediation is an exercise of our baptismal priesthood.

Priesthood of the Faithful

We noted above that St. Paul begins his comments on baptism with the question, "Do you not know . . . " This is a loaded question, one with multiple layers of responses. Our initial remarks on baptism focused on our being plunged into the saving mystery of Christ—his death and resurrection, his self-emptying and exaltation, his poverty of self and fullness of risen life—and our being made members of his very Body. This is so because through baptism the Holy Spirit takes up divine dwelling within us; through this indwelling, we are temples of the Holy Spirit who have God's very life coursing within us. The old self dies and a new self reborn in God's very life emerges.

Another fruit of baptism that has tremendous implications for the identity of the liturgical assembly is that through baptism we are made sharers in the high priesthood of Christ. In the First Letter of Peter we read, "you are a chosen race, a royal priesthood, a holy nation, God's own people . . . " (2:9). In the Letter to the Hebrews chapters five to ten firmly establish that Christ is our high priest and through him we share in the new covenant he mediated (Heb 8:6), a covenant promising that "with our hearts sprinkled clean from an evil conscience and our bodies washed with pure water" (Heb 10:22) it will bring "a great reward" (Heb 10:35). That reward is nothing less than the gift of faith and salvation (Heb 10:39).

By our baptismal sharing in Christ's royal priesthood, we too become mediators of this new covenant with its gift of faith and salvation. We are to let ourselves "be built into a spiritual house, to be a holy priesthood, to offer spiritual sacrifices acceptable to God through Jesus Christ" (1 Pet 2:5). We see here a notion of priesthood that is not limited to ordained, ministerial priesthood, but that is true of all those baptized in Christ. In fact, the use of "priesthood" in the New Testament always refers to the more general priesthood of all the faithful. Through the incarnation the priestly mediation of the Old Testament has ended. Incorporation into Christ means an identity with that same Christ so that church, the community of the assembly at worship, is realized in the exercise of its priesthood. Our priestly identity is a mediation of Christ's risen presence in the church through his Holy Spirit.

We express our priestly identity beyond its visibility as a liturgical assembly. Our priestly mediation is also expressed concretely and visibly by a life of service, understood as our ministry of the Gospel. "God . . . will not overlook your work and the love that you showed for his sake in serving the saints" (Heb 6:10). Our role as sharers in the priesthood of Christ is none other than that of living a Gospel life, a life that proclaims that Christ lives in and through us and his saving work continues. Our daily living proclaims first and foremost a Person: "It is no longer I who live, but it is Christ who lives in me" (Gal 2:20).

Participation of the Faithful

Given our baptismal consecration as sharers in the priesthood of Christ, we celebrate Eucharist, that unparalleled memorial of the paschal mystery, as witnesses to Christ's passing over from death to risen life and our entry into that same passing over. At issue is the participation of the faithful in the liturgical celebration. The ministry of the assembly requires a kind of presence to God and each other that is the identifying factor of a truly dynamic church. This presence, encounter with God, identifies us as God's own.

Participation means far more than being there. Liturgical participation is a dynamic encounter between presence to each other and presence to divine presence. Liturgical participation is dynamic because it seeks conversion—turning from all that keeps us from growing in our self-identity as members of the Body of Christ, turning from anything that is not consistent with Gospel living. Participation calls us to transformation of self so that we become more a "self-in-Christ." The reflection of the next chapter addresses more fully the participation of the faithful in liturgy.

A first determinative statement we can make about the ministry of the assembly is that it is to *be* the Body of Christ, the church made visible. As a liturgical assembly we make visible our baptismal identity and commitment when we respond to God's summons to divine presence, to enact the saving mystery of Christ, that is, the paschal mystery. Our ministry is simply to *be* who we are and who God is transforming us to be ever more.

2

The *Doing* of
the Liturgical Assembly

At first glance thinking about the "doing" of the liturgical assembly might lead us immediately to all the gestures, postures, and actions the assembly does during any given liturgy. This visible "doing" is certainly part of the ministry of the liturgical assembly. But it is only a part, and actually a very small part. The doing always leads to our identity as the assembly, as the church made visible, as the Body united with Christ its Head in the person of the ordained priest. Much more is happening than simply doing when the assembly wholeheartedly participates in the liturgical action.

One of the most oft-quoted phrases of the Second Vatican Council is "full, conscious, and active participation." It seems like more than Catholics have heard this challenge and have responded with attempts to bring about a more lively and welcoming worship experience—one much more "user-friendly." Most parishes have introduced more contemporary music, various musical instruments, liturgical movement (dance), and other full-body, hands-on worship elements. In all this our hearts are in the right place: we want our worship services to touch the individuals who come, facilitate an encounter with the Divine, overflow in praise and thanks, and make a difference in the way we live. There remains a question, however: What did the council really have in mind when the council fathers spoke of a new way to participate in worship?

Catholic liturgy planners and leaders are struggling with what lies underneath this clarion call of the council for full, conscious, and active participation. It simply won't do to have people come to church and be bumps on a log; worship is definitely not a spectator sport! We are concerned about our young people who don't seem interested in established worship patterns. We are scrambling for solutions to the contemporary vs. traditional worship style battles. At the same time, "participation" in worship actually raises some deep issues to which we must attend if we continue on our journey toward salvation. Some of these issues will become clear as we reflect on what it means to participate in liturgy fully, consciously, and actively.

No fewer than five paragraphs in The Constitution on the Sacred Liturgy (*Sacrosanctum Concilium*) address the issue of participation by all the assembly members in liturgy.[1] Only one paragraph, however, uses the complete phrase, "full, conscious, and active participation" (14). One other uses "full, active participation," thus repeating two out of three of the adjectives for participation used in number 14 (see 41). In all other cases the constitution refers only to "active" participation (see 27, 30, and 50). The most interesting paragraph perhaps is number 30, which even lists the envisioned active participation: everyone actively participates through acclamations, responses, psalms, antiphons, hymns, actions, gestures, bodily attitudes, and reverent silence.

This brief survey of data from the constitution raises a simple question: What, really, is intended when we speak of full, conscious, and active participation? Is it simply a fluke of the constitution that only one paragraph mentions all three adjectives for participation? Did the council fathers intend these three adjectives to be synonymous, simply putting three in to bring serious emphasis to their point about participation? It would not seem so.

Active Participation

Active participation in the celebration of liturgy is an expression of the priesthood of all believers that was conferred at baptism. In its deepest sense this "active participation" means no less than the transformation of the assembly into an ever more perfect image of the Body of Christ. Active participation means appropriating—making our own—the paschal ("passing over" from dying to rising) actions of Christ that are the focus of liturgy.

In another and more familiar sense this active participation, which is so much the hallmark of present liturgical renewal, means standing and sitting, singing and gesturing, preparing and ministering. A large number and variety of actions characterize our liturgical ministry. These are concrete expressions of our baptismal priesthood, ways that we mediate God's presence for ourselves and each other.

Active participation means *actively engaging* all those who are present during liturgy. It won't do to have a choir sing all the hymns; at some point the whole assembly must be invited to open with full throats their hearts to God. It won't do to have the presiding priest lead liturgy in such a manner that it is clear he is doing liturgy and the rest are there to watch; liturgical leadership cannot function apart from those who are being led, namely, the whole assembly. In a little different vein, it won't do only to use one's head in a worship service. The Constitution on the Sacred Liturgy also makes clear that the *whole body* must be engaged in worship (30). Particularly interesting is the inclusion of attitudes and silence in the constitution's list of active worship elements (30).

First, let's attend to attitude. Sometimes we are not aware how our attitude affects others: if I am bored, this rubs off; if I am angry, this rubs off; if I am enthusiastic, this rubs off; if I am grateful, this rubs off; if I am filled with praise, this rubs off; if I am genuinely concerned for others when I respond to the intercessions, this rubs off; if I am committed to being there, this rubs off. All of this makes a difference not only by affecting others' participation, but it also affects how we are as the church, the Body of Christ. If one member slacks off in participation, two things simultaneously happen: first, the Body is weakened; second, the others who are participating lift up that slacker. Thus, the attitude of assembly members actually is a give-and-take situation.

Second, let's attend to silence. We might think of silence as a time to do nothing, to vegetate. Silence included with elements of active participation suggests otherwise. In the silence something is to happen *actively*. Silence, in other words, is a time to *do something* (pray, contemplate, encounter) and to *be someone* (creature in stillness before the Creator). Ironically, the moments of silence that are a necessary part of liturgy may well become the most engaging, active participation! Unfortunately, in all too many celebrations of liturgy silence is barely there, and even absent altogether. "Active" participation challenges us to get involved, be engaged, *do* the worship service.

Liturgical gestures. We do any number of things with our bodies during liturgy, most of which we don't even think about. We just do them because that's what we've always done or that is what other members of the assembly are doing. In reality, however, each gesture we make is fraught with meaning.

The *sign of the cross* is the same gesture and words used at baptism. We make the sign of the cross with holy water when we enter the church. We sign ourselves at the very beginning and end of liturgy. This suggests to us that everything that happens in between is the work of the Holy Trinity, is God's work on our behalf. We sign ourselves at the beginning of the proclamation of the gospel, using a different gesture, begging God that these words be in our minds, on our lips, and in our hearts.

When the priest (and deacon) approach the altar at the beginning of Mass and again at the end, he pauses to *kiss the altar*. The altar is consecrated with holy chrism when it is new. Holy chrism is a special oil we use in very few liturgical rites. Each of us is anointed with holy chrism at our baptism (and confirmation) as a sign of our participation in Christ's priesthood. Priests and bishops are anointed with holy chrism at their ordination. The altar and walls of the church are anointed with holy chrism at their consecration and dedication. These anointings set persons and things apart to be special presences of the risen Christ. So, when the priest kisses the altar at the beginning of Mass, he is symbolically kissing Christ. More kissing takes place at Mass! After proclaiming the gospel, the deacon or priest kisses the *Book of the Gospels*, reminding us that Christ is truly present in the proclamation of the gospel (see SC 7).

Sometimes the *Book of the Gospels* is *incensed* before the proclamation. Incensation is an ancient gesture, begging God, to borrow the words of the psalmist, to "Let my prayer be counted as incense before you, / and the lifting up of my hands as an evening sacrifice" (Ps 141:2). As the smoke rises up to heaven, so do we beg that our prayer rise up to God. When incense is used to sanctify the gifts as part of the preparation of the gifts before the Liturgy of the Eucharist, the priest is incensed and so may the people be incensed. We unite ourselves with these gifts, offering them to God, that they may be transformed by the action of the Holy Spirit.

The priest (and sometimes the assembly members) uses his hands a lot. He *extends his hands* over the bread and wine during the eucharistic prayer in what is called an *epiclesis*, a prayer invoking the Holy Spirit to come upon them, using these or similar words, depending upon which eucharistic prayer is used: "Therefore, O Lord, we humbly implore you: / by the same Spirit graciously make holy / these gifts we have brought to you for consecration, / that they may become the Body and Blood / of your Son our Lord Jesus Christ" (Eucharistic Prayer III). The priest *lifts up his hands* in a gesture called the *orans*, which means "praying." The traditional Jewish prayer posture is to raise one's hands to God, as the line from Psalm 141 above says. It is as though we want to "push" our prayer up to God. Raised hands is an open gesture, a kind of surrender of ourselves to God. When the priest prays this way (during the collect, the prayer over the gifts, the eucharistic prayer, and the prayer after Communion) he raises all of our prayers and hearts to God as he prays in the name of the whole assembly. And there is another gesture with the hands that we ourselves make: when receiving

Holy Communion, we don't just grab the Body of Christ. To borrow the words of St. Ambrose, we place one hand within the other to make a throne to receive Christ our King.

After the words of consecration, the priest *elevates* the Body of Christ and then the chalice with the Blood of Christ. These gestures were introduced into Mass around the beginning of the thirteenth century so the people could see the consecrated elements. This was especially important at a time when the laity did not consider themselves worthy actually to receive Holy Communion.

One other gesture needs to be mentioned, that of offering a *sign of peace* to one another, a gesture introduced at the liturgical renewal after Vatican II. Recently the US bishops have decided to keep this gesture at its present position, right before receiving Holy Communion. The context of this exchange, given by the prayer the priest prays just before the sign of peace may be given, is that of the risen Jesus appearing to his disciples. He wishes them peace. It is Christ's peace we exchange, and whether we shake hands (the usual gesture for the US church), embrace, or actually kiss another (appropriate for family members, as an example), it doesn't matter; what matters is that we share Christ's peace because we are one with Christ in his Body, the church.

Conscious Participation

The challenge to "conscious" participation only occurs once in The Constitution on the Sacred Liturgy (14), but this doesn't make it something unimportant or not worth our serious reflection. As the word "conscious" implies, we are speaking here of awareness, of deliberate effort. The very word "conscious" derives from the Latin noun *conscius*, which means having a common knowledge with another, to be privy to.

This word origin suggests, first, that conscious participation involves more than ourselves. In fact, in the very call to celebrate liturgy we are invited to gather and present ourselves before God—ultimately to say *yes* to the divine activity in which we are about to engage ourselves. "Conscious" participation requires of us a *surrender* of ourselves to the worship event.

A second implication of the word origin: since "conscious" is a *common* knowledge, even our yes, our surrender is possible only because of the others who are present with us at liturgy. We can become privy to divine presence only when we surrender ourselves to the bigger action, which is not what we as individuals do, but what God does in us as we do together. The very word "liturgy" comes from two Greek words meaning "the people's work." The real work of liturgy is not so much our active participation (as challenging and demanding as that may well be), as it is the work of *surrendering* ourselves to God's presence and God's action.

Most important, this surrender means that we let go of our individuality—with our likes and dislikes, our needs and desires—and surrender ourselves to be the Body of Christ at worship. Conscious participation in terms of common knowledge is not a matter of gaining a new insight. Rather, common knowledge takes place in our hearts in our surrender to being someone other than our individual selves—our surrender to being the visible, worshiping Body of Christ. Conscious participation challenges us to surrender to being the Body of Christ where God works through us and within us.

This kind of conscious surrender, wholehearted yes to God and divine presence and action, requires of us a most profound kind of humility. Again, word origins can guide our reflection. Humility comes from the Latin word *humus*, meaning ground, earth, soil. The second creation account tells us that God created human beings "from the dust of the ground" (Gen 2:7). Humility does not mean putting oneself down; it is not self-deprecation; it is not denying our gifts and talents. True humility is acknowledging who God made us to be. True humility is acting consistently with our true being. True humility is opening ourselves to God's continuing, creating goodness toward us. Surrendering ourselves to the liturgical action is to say yes to allowing God to take us and transform us. True humility is opening ourselves to God's action of making us more perfect members of the Body of Christ.

Liturgical postures. All postures we assume at Mass express our profound humility and surrender to God's action in the liturgy. Postures express our conscious participation in liturgy, especially when we do them deliberately and beautifully.

The most profound and humble posture at liturgy is *prostration*. This is an act of total surrender, whereby one stretches out on the ground (floor) before God. It occurs rarely and during special liturgical moments. On Good Friday it is the posture the clergy assume after they process into the assembly in silence. At ordinations and at some religious professions the candidates prostrate themselves during the singing of the Litany of All Saints. Prostration is a posture of total surrender.

Kneeling is also a posture expressing humility. On our knees before God, we beg for God to hear our prayer. Kneeling is a posture of submission, of saying yes. It is a posture of penance and confession. It is a posture of adoration and reverence. We kneel at solemn moments of the liturgy; in the United States, kneeling is the posture we take during the eucharistic prayer from after the Holy, Holy, Holy until after the great amen (see GIRM 43). Some people kneel after receiving Holy Communion as a posture of adoration. A variation of kneeling is *genuflecting*, during which the right knee is bent to touch the floor (see GIRM 174). We genuflect before the Blessed Sacrament reserved. Like kneeling, it is a gesture of humility, adoration, and reverence.

Standing is a posture expressing respect, readiness, praise. During the Liturgy of the Word we are seated for the first two readings and responsorial psalm; but we stand for the proclamation of the gospel out of respect for Christ, who is present in his word, and as a sign of our readiness and eagerness to hear Christ's word and encounter his presence in the very proclamation of the gospel. We also (in the United States) stand to receive Holy Communion, a posture that combines both respect and praise during this sacred exchange (see GIRM 160). After a brief time of adoration after Holy Communion we stand for the concluding rites, indicating our readiness to disassemble as a worshiping community before God and take up the individual challenge to live the liturgy we have celebrated. We stand for the *Gloria* and the Holy, Holy, Holy as we raise our hearts and voices in praise of God.

Sitting is a posture of repose, receptivity, meditation. We sit during the first two readings to receive and internalize the word of God that is proclaimed. We sit during the preparation of the gifts and altar, and when we are not singing a hymn, the time is a real gift for meditating on what we have heard, professed, and prayed for during the Liturgy of the Word. We sit during the brief period of silence after Holy Communion and in our quiet repose adore the risen Christ whom we have just received into our being.

There are usually four *processions* during a typical Sunday celebration of the Eucharist: the entrance procession, procession with the gospel book, the presentation of gifts, and the communion procession. Processions are always a symbol of movement, transition, change. We begin in one place, and end up someplace else. Even though the members of the assembly all are not directly involved in the processions except for the Communion one, if one member of the Body acts, the whole body acts. Most often the processions are accompanied by hymns, and by singing we do directly participate in a procession, if not in the actual movement. At the entrance procession we move from being members of the Body of Christ to being church made visible; we move from being individuals to being a community before God. At the presentation of gifts we move from giving of our gifts for the sacrament and for the poor to placing ourselves on the altar as a living sacrifice to be transformed by God, receiving from God the transformed gifts we have brought. During the gospel procession we anticipate the presence of Christ in the proclamation of his word as we physically, when appropriate, turn ourselves toward the ambo; a rubric now states, "Those present turn towards the ambo as a sign of special reverence for the Gospel of Christ" (GIRM 133). In the communion procession we move (preferably) forward toward the altar, toward the messianic banquet where we receive and are nourished by the heavenly food God gives us. This processional movement already takes us to the anticipated fulfillment of our baptismal journey, where one day we will enjoy the fullness of life forever.

Another gesture that is specified for the assembly is *bowing* at certain times. When entering a church where the Blessed Sacrament is kept in a separate reservation chapel, we bow to the altar as a sign of reverence. We bow our heads at the name of Jesus.

We bow during the Creed at the words describing the conception and incarnation of Jesus (see GIRM 137, 275). If there are no kneelers in the place of worship, and the posture during the entire eucharistic prayer is standing, then we bow after each elevation when the priest genuflects (see GIRM 43). We bow in reverence before receiving the Body and Blood of Christ (see GIRM 160).

Before leaving this brief outline of liturgical postures, it is fitting to mention other acts the assembly does, although they would not seem at first glance to be "postures." The assembly is to enter into the liturgical celebration as the one Body of Christ (see SC 26), but also with each individual's whole body. Liturgy is very physical and uses all the senses. Our singing, responding, and praying are all ways to participate more completely in the liturgy. To hold back is to diminish the Body.

Full Participation

Two paragraphs of the constitution mention "full" participation (14 and 41), but give us little clue about what the council bishops had in mind. We might take our clue from our previous two reflections. Active engagement and conscious surrender both take us beyond ourselves. As characteristics of our liturgical participation, they render us able to allow God to work within us. Full participation, then, has to do with how God *transforms* us through the worship event into being more perfect members of the Body of Christ. Full participation has to do with our openness and receptivity to the transforming grace God offers us.

Liturgy involves a bidirectional giving. We give God ourselves through praise and thanks; God gives us a share in divine life, which transforms us into an ever-deepening identity as members of the Body of Christ. Participation reaches its apex when God transforms us. Thus, liturgy is always a "life-threatening experience": through our engagement and surrender God makes us other than who we are when we begin liturgy. Interestingly enough, while we often think of liturgy as what we give God, full participation implies that the most important gift of liturgy is what God gives to us. This does not mean that our gifts are not important—either of the offering or of ourselves—for they are! It does mean that God, who receives our sincere and true gifts, transforms them with divine life.

Moreover, this transformation of ourselves at worship is not simply for our own sake. Indeed, this transformation is precisely what enables us to be sent forth from liturgy to transform our broken and fractured world as we ourselves are transformed. Full participation, then, thrusts us toward mission. We are transformed in order to continue Jesus' saving ministry. "Full" participation challenges us to be transformed by God into ever more perfect members of the Body of Christ; as we are transformed, so is our world transformed. While the work of transformation is wholly God's, we must open ourselves to receive the transforming life God offers us.

It is awesome to think that at liturgy we grow ever more deeply into the divine life that God offers us as a free gift. The ministry of the assembly is to participate actively, consciously, and fully. As we grow into our ability to do just that, we move along our journey toward eschatological (referring to final glory at the end of time) fullness. Liturgy always joins us to the heavenly liturgy (see SC 8), where we stand with all the angels and saints in their eternal song of praise before the throne of God's majesty. Surrendering ourselves to the liturgical action, then, is truly a little bit of heaven. As in heaven, we are drawn to God's presence, to God's divine being. During liturgy we seek God, we encounter God. Ultimately all the singing and praying, postures and gestures of liturgy are for the purpose of tasting and seeing (see Ps 34) the God who is good to us beyond measure.

Anamnesis and offering. At one time we called the beginning of the Liturgy of the Eucharist and before the eucharistic prayer the "offertory." Now we refer to this transition time as the presentation and preparation of the gifts. The reason for this change in terminology is that the offering actually takes place during the eucharistic prayer, after the institution narrative (the recounting of the Last Supper that is part of every eucharistic prayer). So, for example, in Eucharistic Prayer II we pray, "Therefore, as we celebrate / the memorial of his Death and Resurrection, / we offer you, Lord, / the Bread of Life and the Chalice of salvation, / giving thanks that you have held us worthy / to be in your presence and minister to you." Much is happening in this short prayer.

First, we *remember* Jesus' death and resurrection. In Greek, "remember" is the word *anamnesis*. This remembering, however, is not simply a recalling of a past historical event. Liturgical *anamnesis* is a wholly present act in which the meaning and import of what we are remembering is in the present, happening now. The self-offering of Jesus on the cross and his exaltation at the resurrection are, indeed, happening in this very liturgical celebration when Jesus ceaselessly gives himself over to his Father for our salvation.

Second, we are counted worthy to be in God's presence as ministers not because of any act of our own, but because we are one with the divine Son who is being *offered*. And if the Son is offered, so are we. Our ministry as assembly is to offer ourselves along with the risen Christ (see GIRM 79f.). And just as Christ's self-offering is unceasing, so must ours be. Our surrender to God's transforming action in the eucharistic prayer is our offering of ourselves at this moment during liturgy as a pledge of our self-offering and as a commitment to a Gospel way of living.

Acclamations. This term is generally applied to the responses that the assembly makes, even including their amens. The *acclamations* and responses "constitute that level of active participation that is to be made by the assembled faithful in every form of the Mass, so that the action of the whole community may be clearly expressed and fostered" (GIRM 35). Our verbal responses, then, are not to be merely mumbled, without much thought, rote reactions. They affirm our surrender to the liturgical action.

Four acclamations are particularly important. The gospel acclamation is the way "the gathering of the faithful welcomes and greets the Lord who is about to speak to them in the Gospel and profess their faith" (GIRM 62) by singing with full voice. There are three acclamations during the eucharistic prayer, which certainly point to the utter centrality of this prayer. Each acclamation concludes a major section of the prayer. The *Sanctus* (Holy,

Holy, Holy) concludes the preface, the memorial acclamation concludes the institution narrative, and the great amen concludes the whole prayer and, specifically, the doxology. Preferably these acclamations are sung so that greater solemnity and voice can be given to them. They are our affirmation and appropriation of the liturgical action.

3

The *Why* of
the Liturgical Assembly

Let's admit it: most of us go to Sunday Mass without think-ing too much about why and what we are about. As we learn more about liturgy in general and Mass in particular, we soon discover that more happens than we bargain for. Liturgy upends us, challenges us, transforms us. Liturgy upends us when we open ourselves to the life God offers us as a free gift, overflow-ing with wonder and potency. Liturgy challenges us when we surrender ourselves to divine presence. Liturgy transforms us when we willingly receive the depth of the richness of divine life God offers to us. The "why" of the liturgical assembly is about celebrating the holiness God is and shares with us.

Called to Holiness

"Speak to all the congregation of the people of Israel and say to them: You shall be holy, for I the LORD your God am holy" (Lev 19:2a). This is just one of the instances in what is called the "holiness code" of the book of Leviticus (chaps. 17–26), where we are summoned to be holy. Why? Because God is holy and God calls us to be a chosen people who embody divine love and care, compassion and mercy, forgiveness and reconciliation. God is holy and desires us to be holy.

Sometimes our mental image of holiness is of the saints pictured on holy cards. They have angelic faces and look as if they never did anything but pray and be in communion with God. And certainly they never sin. Actually, this is not a good picture of the saints, and not a good way to think of our being holy. The saints struggled just as we do with discerning and doing God's will. This can give us courage. We are holy when we respond to God's overtures of love and are faithful in doing God's will. God doesn't count so much the times we fail but rejoices more in the times we are faithful (see Luke 15:7).

Holiness is the very essence of who God is: "Holy, holy, holy is the LORD of hosts; / the whole earth is full of his glory" (Isa 6:3). We cannot see God's holiness but do see its manifestation: glory. God loves so much that God's being, God's holiness cannot be contained. God chooses to infuse us with divine holiness, divine life, and in that choice calls us to be God's one people: "You shall be holy to me; for I the LORD am holy, and I have separated you from the other peoples to be mine" (Lev 20:26).

Our holiness is a matter of responding to God's call, of being in communion with God, of having God's life in us. We cannot see our own holiness, but we do recognize our being in a graced relationship with God because that is manifested in the way we live. When we do good, we are manifesting God's (and our) holiness. When we love, we are manifesting God's holiness. When we forgive, show mercy, reconcile, we are manifesting God's holiness. Our daily living manifests the holiness with which God has gifted us and manifests God's presence and glory: "As God's chosen ones, holy and beloved, clothe yourselves with compassion, kindness, humility, meekness, and patience. . . . And let the peace of Christ rule in your hearts, to which indeed you were called in the one body. And be thankful" (Col 3:12, 15).

Holiness is not a pie-in-the-sky concept; it is a life to be lived. To be holy as God is holy means that we must have the same mind as the divine Son: "Let the same mind be in you that was in Christ Jesus . . . [He] emptied himself" (Phil 2:5, 7). Jesus emptied himself in becoming incarnate to live among us as one of us; he emptied himself during his public ministry; he emptied himself in his self-giving at the Last Supper; he emptied himself in the Garden of Gethsemane by surrendering himself to his Father's will; he emptied himself on the cross by embracing death; he emptied himself after the resurrection by continuing to instruct his disciples; he emptied himself by leaving his saving mission in the hands of his followers. All this emptying of self, all this self-giving, manifests Jesus' holiness. Our own holiness must be characterized by our own emptying of ourselves, by our own daily self-giving.

Being holy is a pure and gracious gift of God. It is a response to God's presence. But it isn't exactly a free gift. The gift has its demands. If we are to be holy like God, then our lives must reflect the continual conversion to which holiness and liturgy call us. The transformation that God works in us during liturgy must be carried beyond the rite itself into daily living. The liturgical assembly makes visible and present the whole church; our lives make visible and present our oneness in the Body of Christ when we live consistently with Gospel values. Liturgy itself reminds us of this call to lived holiness when we are dismissed at the end of Mass. Two dismissal formulae express this so well: "Go and announce the Gospel of the Lord"; "Go in peace, glorifying the Lord by your life." What beautiful words with which to be sent forth! What demanding words!

The dismissal at the end of Mass is not simply a kind of wave of the hand with an attitude of "get out of here and get on with it." The dismissal at the end of Mass is truly a beginning. It is ultimately an invitation to take our ministry of the assembly to our daily living and continue being the Body of Christ with all of its holiness. The dismissal is an invitation to continue Jesus' saving mission—no small task, indeed!

Jesus' Saving Mission

Salvation is an easily misunderstood term. All too often it is thought of as the rather narrow endeavor of doing whatever we need to do in life to avoid hell and be admitted into heaven (even if with a detour in purgatory). While it is true that our entire Christian journey is about coming to fullness of God's holiness and life in eternity, much more is at stake along the way than simply avoiding evil. Coming to salvation is an enlargement of self.

The word "salvation" comes from the Hebrew word that has the same root as the name Jesus. This word is *yesha* and it originally did not have a specifically religious meaning at all. It meant to be enlarged, to be spacious, vast. When God "saved" Israel of old, God brought them from slavery to freedom, brought them to the promised land that was vast land overflowing with abundance. With freedom and abundance, Israel experienced the possibility of wholeness of being, a healthy relationship with God. The only thing that kept Israel from enjoying this divine favor was their own obstinacy, their own rejection of the terms of their covenantal relationship with God. When Israel allowed God to be the center of their lives and wills, they were prosperous and lived in peace. When they focused on themselves and their petty ambitions, then they experienced God's punishment, usually at the hands of their enemies.

Jesus' advent into our human condition brought a new covenant with its new possibilities for relationship with him and his Father. The health and wholeness of salvation are now centered on Christ Jesus who came to deliver us from the slavery of sin into the marvelous light of risen life. Jesus, "savior," unites us to be one with him and in that unity opens up for us the vast richness of life in Christ. At Mass the assembly encounters their Christ, is transformed by God's grace, and is sent forth to live this transformation. That is, we are sent forth to live as Body of Christ, to live the Gospel the divine Son taught us.

The ministry of the assembly is to be faithful to the enlargement of self that is identity with Christ. The ministry of the assembly is to become more than we are. Not by our work alone. We surrender to God's action of transformation. We give ourselves over to who God is calling us to be. A lifelong, faithful journey of surrender and transformation is the road to salvation.

Jesus is the Way, the Truth, and the Life (see John 14:1-14). Jesus is the unwavering Way to the fullness of life because he is one with his Father. Jesus is the Truth because he never deviated from doing his Father's will. He is the Life because, through his obedience even to death on the cross, he conquered sin and evil, was exalted at the resurrection, and sends his Spirit to dwell within and among us, an indwelling that is the very same divine life.

Relationship of Liturgy, Self, and World

Liturgy forms self in the likeness of Christ; because of that likeness we can transform the world. Who we are is the risen presence of Christ. Let's make three simple points about the relationship of liturgy, self, and world. But let's make them clearly and boldly.

First, being in healthy relationship demands a *just* relationship. Justice that lasts and makes a difference is more than "ethical" or "retributive" or "distributive" justice. These are theological terms and may be helpful, but they are not persuasive enough. The justice to which we are called by Scripture and liturgy is a pervading and invading justice. It is one that quickens to the very core of our being, making a difference in us and, therefore, in the world in which we live. This justice is measured by right relationships with God, self, others, world.

Sometimes the "just person" is thought to be the one working directly with the poor, a missionary in a third-world country, or someone publicly trying to heal the ills of society. While this activity is important, it can mislead us and entice us to forget that our very baptism sets us in a relationship of identity: we are, together, the Body of Christ. What we do to one is done to all and, most important, is done to Christ (see Matt 25). Who we are to one, we are to all. We are *all* called to live justly and in right relationship. It is upon this that we will be judged. It is upon this that we will enter into the fullness of life for all eternity.

What must be clear is that this kind of justice—being in right relationship with Other and others—is not a matter of specific acts, but of a way of living. Justice as right relationship means that we begin all our relationships with each other out of the conviction that all have an inherent dignity simply because they live. Recognizing the dignity of others necessarily shapes the way we relate. It means that there can be many differences, but always the same respect for dignity. Differences don't necessarily divide; they cause ruptures when we lose sight of each other's inherent dignity.

Second, we don't celebrate liturgy to *hear* about how we should be in right relationship, but to *celebrate* that reality in our lives. In other words, celebrating liturgy (on the one hand) and being just and doing justice (on the other hand) aren't two separate domains, but two dimensions of the one reality we live. If our lives are not marked by right relationships, how can we truly celebrate liturgy? We are not talking about a dualism between the spiritual and material, between God's world and our own. Justice calls us to live what we celebrate and to celebrate what we live.

Third, justice isn't what someone does "out there" with the clearly disadvantaged (as important as that is). Justice is the expression of who we are as baptized, committed Christians. It is not what we leave to the "professional" missionaries or social workers but is constitutive of who we are as members of the Body of Christ. Ultimately, what counts is what *each of us* undertakes concerning right relationships. The world will not truly be whole (be saved) until each of us looks deeply inside ourselves and sets right all of our relationships.

Let our liturgies summon us to a transformation in ourselves that makes a difference in how we are with God, self, others, world. Our greatest amen is our life-living liturgy.

4

The *Place* of
the Liturgical Assembly

The assembly space is the largest space in the church building. It is called a "nave" from the Latin *navis*, meaning "ship." During an earlier time of the church, the spaces for worship were often built to resemble sailing ships, signaling that the church is on the sea of life, journeying toward the health and wholeness of salvation. The nave of the church building symbolized the ship's deck where the sailors and passengers could gather. As the members of the Body of Christ gathered in the nave, they were reminded that they are on their journey of salvation, their journey toward everlasting life.

As time went on, both the understanding of liturgy and the spirituality of the Body of Christ changed, and the worship space was constructed to reflect this. In churches built before Vatican II, the place of the liturgical assembly was quite clear: in the main body of the church, separated from the sanctuary space by a communion rail. The seating was in neat rows, everyone facing forward toward the sanctuary space, the holy space where the holy action took place. The altar was fixed against the apse, an architectural feature consisting of a semicircular wall with a dome over it, often facing east. An east-west axis was favored for the orientation of church buildings and this carried rich symbolism.

People entered church from the west, the region of darkness (and sin); coming into church, they left behind their sinful lives to come into a magnificently beautiful building reminding them of heaven. They faced east during the liturgical celebration, the region of light, resurrection, and life. The architecture of church buildings before Vatican II included spires, vaulted ceilings, and high arches, which lifted the eyes (and hearts) upward, where God dwelt in the heavens. These buildings were inspiring and glorious, monuments to the faith and generosity of the people. Many of these older churches remain today, renovated to serve the renewed liturgy. But the main features often remain: forward-facing seating and clearly defined people and clergy spaces.

Much architectural experimentation has taken place since Vatican II in order to reflect the renewal called for by The Constitution on the Sacred Liturgy. The altar is no longer fixed against an apse (most often, this architectural feature is not even part of newly built churches) but is now freestanding and the presider faces the people. Often there are chairs instead of pews, which are more comfortable, allow for flexibility, and generally increase seating capacity. The configuration of the assembly is often in the round or fan shaped. Instead of everyone looking forward to the altar with the exclusion of everything and everyone else, the different configuration allows for the members of the assembly to interact better. This is not simply a newfangled idea but is fraught with symbolism.

Configuration of the Assembly

How we are together affects the unfolding of liturgical celebration. How we are together radically affects the full, conscious, and active participation of the assembly. How we are together affects the sense of liturgy as a communal celebration of the Body of Christ. Many of us experience daily Mass with twenty or so people in a building with seating for six hundred. Often the participants are scattered all over the church, far apart from each other. Instead of a communal celebration, there is a risk that liturgy becomes private devotion. To redress this situation many new church buildings have day chapels that are much smaller in size, less expensive to heat or air condition, and far more conducive to a sense of community.

The ministry of the assembly includes ministry to each other. When we are isolated by seating configuration, too large a space, or other kinds of barriers, it is difficult to grasp that liturgy is truly a communal event. Some people object that seeing others during Mass is distracting. Perhaps this objection points to how little understanding we have of ourselves as the Body of Christ; how little regard we have for the inherent dignity of others; and how little we understand full, conscious, and active participation. Rather than a distraction, other people are fellow pilgrims on our journey toward salvation. We journey to eternal life together.

The configuration of the assembly is often not the culprit when people distract each other. Often the culprit is that people have not truly surrendered themselves to the liturgical action. Sometimes this is because there has not been enough attentiveness to preparation, both long-term in our daily living as well as immediate preparation before Mass begins. Thank God we have done away with the absolute, rigid silence in church that was the rule before Vatican II. It is entirely appropriate to quietly greet one another when finding our place in church. We recall Jesus' promise, "For where two or three are gathered in my name, I am there among them" (Matt 18:20; see GIRM 27). Before Mass ought not to be a raucous time, however. At a reasonable time before the entrance procession begins, "it is a praiseworthy practice for silence to be observed in the church, in the sacristy, in the vesting room, and in adjacent areas, so that all may dispose themselves to carry out the sacred celebration in a devout and fitting manner" (GIRM 45).

Discomfort with assembly configuration might come from two different directions. On the one hand, a "theater" style of seating (with everyone in rows facing forward) might make having a sense of being the Body of Christ very difficult. On the other hand, seating in the round or in a fan shape might focus the assembly members too much on themselves, diminishing some of the reverence and sacredness of what is taking place.

Another issue here is a misunderstanding about what liturgical prayer is. Liturgical prayer—the celebration of the seven sacraments and the Liturgy of the Hours—is different from devotional prayer. Liturgical prayer is ritual enactment of the paschal mystery that is a continuation of the ministry of Jesus. Liturgical prayer is highly governed by the church precisely because of what is at stake—the enactment of Jesus' saving mystery in the here and now. Devotional prayer is all our prayer that is not liturgical prayer and "should be so drawn up that they harmonize with the liturgical seasons, accord with the sacred liturgy, are in some way derived from it, and lead the people to it, since in fact the liturgy by its very nature is far superior to any of them" (SC 13). In a real sense, our daily, devotional prayer is a kind of preparation for liturgy. Devotional prayer puts us in the presence of God and helps us become more attentive to divine encounters.

Liturgical centers. Liturgical centers are focal points where specific liturgical actions take place. For Mass, the liturgical centers are three: the *altar*, of course; the *presider's chair*; and the *ambo*, a word derived from the Greek word meaning "reading table," which is the place from where the Scriptures are proclaimed as well as possibly the responsorial psalm, homily, and prayer of the faithful (see GIRM 309). When baptisms take place, the *baptismal font* is a liturgical center. In a cathedral there is the *cathedra* (from the Greek meaning "chair"), the special chair for the bishop, his "seat of authority."

Sacred spaces. Any church building has a number of separate spaces designated for specific purposes. The *sanctuary*, while perhaps not so clearly set off as before the council, nonetheless is its own space. The sanctuary is the space enveloping the altar, ambo, and presider's chair and those who minister at these liturgical centers. Nothing ought to get in the way of the sight lines to these liturgical centers. The *nave* is the assembly space and is generally the largest sacred space. The *narthex* is the entrance or gathering space where the hospitality ministers greet those coming to liturgy, where the baptismal font may be placed, and leads to the *nave*. The *reconciliation room* is a sacred space where the sacrament of penance is celebrated with an individual; it is larger than the familiar confessional boxes in older churches and permits face-to-face confession. There may be a separate *Blessed Sacrament* chapel where the sacrament is reserved in the tabernacle (a locked and immovable receptacle; see GIRM 314) for Communion for the sick and homebound, for *Viaticum* (Holy Communion for the dying), and for adoration. There may be separate *devotional spaces* with statues or sacred art that promote veneration of the saints and further people's devotional life. A practical space is the *sacristy* and sometimes separate *vesting room*, usually off the sanctuary space and sometimes near the narthex where the entrance procession would begin; here, the ministers vest, and vestments and other things needed for liturgy are stored.

Rich Symbols

Symbols play on us. They affect us. They draw us into themselves and open up for us whole worlds of new meanings and possibilities. Symbols by their nature are not clearly understood. We grasp or engage a symbol at one level, but there are layers and layers of meaning or intent still to tease out. This is why we don't tire, for example, of good art; each time we gaze on a piece something new comes to us. It seems as though the piece is inexhaustible in its depth of communication. Symbols share something (its medium, shape, color, texture, etc.) with the message or intent that they convey.

Liturgical colors are good examples of symbols. They were not arbitrarily chosen but eventually became part of liturgical celebrations around the end of the first millennium (more on colors in the next chapter). So, a symbol points beyond itself, is inexhaustible in meaning and intent, and isn't arbitrary but already shares in the sense of mystery it conveys.

Because symbols play on us, being attentive to symbols is part of the ministry of the assembly. Symbols help to place us within the liturgical action. Liturgy puts to use many symbols, some essential or primary, and others secondary (but not unimportant). Primary symbols of liturgy, of course, are objects and gestures without which we would not have liturgy. Water, for example, is not arbitrary for the celebration of baptism. Without water, one cannot be baptized. Water symbolizes for us two fruits of baptism: we are plunged into the death-dealing waters where the old self dies; we are raised up out of those same waters and receive new life, slaking our thirst for God. Bread and wine are the primary symbols for the Eucharist: these products of nature and human making are changed into the very Body and Blood of the risen Christ, the Bread of Life (see John 6). Holy chrism is the primary symbol for confirmation (and is also used during holy orders and the dedication of a church and consecration of an altar), a fragrant mixture of (usually) olive oil and balsam whereby the anointing reminds us of our strength from the Holy Spirit and that we are consecrated, set apart, to be the presence of Christ for all we meet. In the sacrament of penance the priest extends his hands over the penitent as a symbol of the Holy Spirit coming upon the person and the mercy and forgiveness of God. The sacrament of the anointing of the sick uses a different holy oil, the oil of the sick, to anoint those who ask for and need the special healing balm that Jesus offers. The primary symbol of the sacrament of marriage is the exchange of vows binding the bride and groom to a holy covenant with each other and God.

Besides these primary symbols, many secondary symbols are used during liturgy, some of them more prominent and important than others. Every celebration of Mass requires an altar cross "with the figure of Christ crucified upon it" that is visible to the assembly (GIRM 308).[1] If the altar crucifix is fixed and permanent (e.g., a large one hanging on a wall), this need be the only crucifix in sight (care must be taken not to multiply symbols; see GIRM 318) and then the processional cross need not have a figure of Christ crucified on it (see GIRM 122). If the processional cross is also the altar cross, then it must have a figure of Christ crucified and is placed in a stand or bracket in the sanctuary space visible to all. If a stand for the cross is used, care should be taken that the cross fits snugly in the stand so it stands up straight, but not so tight that it is overly difficult to put in the stand or remove.

Other sacred objects used during liturgy can function as symbols. The paten (small, flat "plate" for holding the large host) and ciborium (a covered vessel, or other similar kinds of vessels) hold the consecrated Hosts. The chalice and communion cups hold the Precious Blood. Ashes are imposed on the forehead on Ash Wednesday as a sign of who we are (made from the dust of the earth) and how our penance during Lent ought to be shaped (to repent and live the Gospel). Candles at one time were primarily functional; before electric lights they enabled those present at liturgy to see and read. Now candles are primarily symbolic; they remind us of Christ who is the Light of the world, dispelling the darkness of sin and evil. Besides the altar candles there are processional candles, the Easter or paschal candle, and baptismal candles.

The *Book of the Gospels* may be carried in the entrance procession and at the gospel procession. Because the proclamation of the gospel is a presence of Christ, the *Book of the Gospels* is afforded all the dignity that we might offer Christ himself: its procession may be accompanied by lighted candles, we bow to it, we hear its proclamation while standing, we sign it with the cross, and it may be incensed (see GIRM 133 and 134). In some churches it is permanently enthroned in a place of honor so that it might be venerated outside of Mass.

For some people vestments may seem quite antiquated and useless. Yet, they have a very important symbolic value. The alb (from the Latin *albus*, white) is the long, white garment worn by the clergy and, in some liturgical communities, by other ministers (see GIRM 119). It is reminiscent of the Roman toga, but for us it has a deep symbolism. At baptism the neophyte (literally, "newly lighted," or those who have just been baptized) is clothed in a white garment. In practice this might be a white shoulder covering or other kind of cloth, but historically this was a full covering, the alb. It symbolized the purity and new life of those who have been baptized into Christ. We have so closely identified the alb with the clergy that, unfortunately, it has largely lost its baptismal symbolism. Perhaps we need to rethink the kind of white garment with which we clothe the newly baptized.

Obviously, all assembly members do not wear an alb, although the importance of their ministry might suggest the appropriateness of this. Something as seemingly insignificant as the attire of the assembly affects the beauty and solemnity of liturgy. At one time dressing for Mass wasn't an issue; one always put on one's "Sunday best." Men came to church in suits and ties and women in hats and gloves. In today's more relaxed North American society, dressing up simply isn't part of our usual routine. Yet we know that dress directly affects our attitudes and comportment. A beautifully (but not necessarily expensively!) dressed assembly is an effective way to express the ministry of the assembly and that the people who gather understand what they are doing as a most important activity.

> **Other liturgical vestments.** The priest and deacon wear a *stole*: the priest around his neck, the deacon from over the left shoulder to his right hip. The stole probably has its roots in the scarf worn by Roman soldiers, marking their rank and office. The *chasuble* is worn by the priest and is the colorful outer garment. It probably has its roots in the outer garment worn in the Roman Empire. The *dalmatic* is worn by the deacon and is similar in purpose to the chasuble but slightly different in design, having "sleeves." The *humeral veil* is a long, wide piece of fabric (usually white) the priest or deacon wears when blessing the people during Benediction with the Blessed Sacrament and also when carrying the Blessed Sacrament in procession. The *cope* is worn by the priest or deacon during Benediction and other solemn rights; it is a long, flowing vestment worn over the shoulders and clasped in the front.

Assembly and Piety

Whether at liturgical celebrations or private prayer, assembly members deport themselves with piety, that is, with reverence, awe, and openness. The word "piety" comes from the Latin *pietas*, meaning "dutiful." It is our right and duty to be before our God in adoration. Notice the opening words of our prefaces: "It is truly right and just, our duty and our salvation, / always and everywhere to give you thanks, / Lord, holy Father, almighty and eternal God, / through Christ our Lord." Our piety is always directed to God with the sentiments owed to our Creator and Redeemer: reverence, awe, love, thanksgiving, praise.

Sometimes people decry the renewed liturgy as lacking piety and reverence. The problem is not with the new liturgy as it is described in The Constitution on the Sacred Liturgy and subsequent liturgical documents. The problem lies with how we do liturgy. The ministry of the assembly includes a responsibility to come to liturgy with the right attitudes, to celebrate it with the right piety, and to live it with the right commitment.

Proper deportment at liturgy by each assembly member affects all other members. If someone is bored, uninterested, not responding, it affects those around her or him. If someone is not careful about the way she or he stands, sits, kneels, processes, it affects those around her or him. If someone comes to liturgy prepared and ready, eager to enter into the liturgical action, then that affects the others in the assembly. We rub off on each other. Deportment is actually a ministry of the assembly! Piety places us in the presence of God and witnesses to our willingness to surrender to God's action within and among us during liturgy. Piety is our orientation toward God, our commitment to openness, our acknowledgment that God is the center of our life.

5

A *Spirituality* of
the Liturgical Assembly

More than once in the previous chapters we have mentioned that the ministry of the liturgical assembly does not end when Mass ends but continues into daily living by making present Christ's saving mystery. This chapter explores this statement in more depth.

A call to ministry reminds us that it is through no merit of our own that we are gifted for the sake of the community. It also reminds us that our responding is not so much simply a matter of making a choice as it is an expression of our baptismal commitment. Ministry is a response to God's lavishing gifts upon us. Ministry is basically a spirituality, a way of living. The spirituality underlying all ministry is rooted in baptism. As such, the exercise of the ministry of the assembly urges regular reflection on the faith commitment out of which this ministry is exercised. Without this deep spiritual value, rooted in our baptism, ministry loses its sense of serving God in each other. But when ministry is an expression of our own loving response to a loving God, ministry itself is a sign of God's presence and the kingdom come.

The impetus for the ministry of the assembly derives from the depth of the liturgical experience, not from observable characteristics of the assembly (even though they are indicators and, as such, cannot be lightly dismissed). This is to say that what makes liturgy, liturgy (communal, ecclesial, transforming, enacting Christ's saving mystery, encounter/response to divine presence, eschatological, mission-giving) is that which makes the spirituality of the assembly. The spirituality of the assembly is a liturgical spirituality. To push this further, good liturgy always leads to authentic liturgical spirituality; good liturgical celebration is also a celebration of Christian living. On the other hand, the celebration of liturgy that does not lead to living a liturgical spirituality is empty or unfruitful.

Ultimately, the issue at stake is the relationship between liturgy and a lived spirituality, between assembly as Body of Christ and world, which is to say that what is at stake is the relation between liturgy and life. Is liturgy something to which we go, or is liturgy a celebration of what it means to be baptized and truly live that commitment? Essential for an authentic spirituality of the liturgical assembly is that our spirituality be ecclesial (from and to the church), an act of remembering, and mission oriented.

First of all, the spirituality of the liturgical assembly is an *ecclesial* spirituality. Unlike devotional spiritualities that are embraced by only a segment of the church and disclose a particular aspect of the mystery we live and celebrate, liturgical spirituality is that of the entire church by virtue of the common identity we share because of our baptism. Plunged into the saving mystery of Christ, we embrace who and what the church is: the manifestation of the risen Christ for all people at all times. This is who the liturgical assembly is and how they are called to live.

Second, the spirituality of the liturgical assembly is an act of *remembering* God's saving deeds on our behalf through the life and ministry of Jesus Christ. Liturgical spirituality, then, is always a reflection of the paschal mystery lived in the here and now. Embracing a liturgical spirituality is hardly a mere psychological act or emotional escape valve. Liturgical spirituality demands of us no less than entering into the death into which Jesus himself entered, an act that conquered death and brought risen life. Liturgical spirituality bids us to live prayerfully, united with God at all times through the Spirit. Liturgical spirituality is a spiritual way of living the paschal mystery; it is the reality of living as Jesus did with all its consequences, the main one being the demand for our daily self-emptying for the good of others.

A third essential for the spirituality of the assembly is that it always implies a *mission*: being sent to do God's will as Jesus did. Liturgical spirituality, then, always has ethical and justice-seeking implications. Just as Eucharist transforms us into something more, so does liturgical spirituality impel us to transform our world into something more. Celebrating liturgy and living a liturgical spirituality ought to make a difference. When both good liturgy and its correlative, liturgical spirituality, have taken hold of a liturgical community, we just may hear again the exclamations, "See how they love one another!" (Tertullian, an early Christian writer) and "There was not a needy person among them" (Acts 4:34). This happens, and liturgical spirituality is nourished, when we celebrate truly good liturgy.

Good Liturgy

What is good liturgy? This is a good question to ask ourselves on occasion because it prompts us to examine our presuppositions and consider what it is we expect and do when we celebrate liturgy. It goes without saying that only "good" liturgy spawns authentic liturgical spirituality.

Good liturgy is not so easy to tack down. Different people may have different ideas about what characteristics combine to make good liturgy, and often people feel very strong about this. A few thoughts are immediately obvious: good liturgy isn't necessarily that which appeals to us, isn't always a matter of "satisfying" us (in the sense of giving us good feelings), doesn't cater to whims and fancies, isn't stagnant or unchangeable. In other words, good liturgy doesn't depend upon the ideas of one or a few individuals, but it is liturgy that reflects the tradition of celebrations in the church and thereby makes present the paschal mystery, transforming us into ever more perfect images of the Body of Christ.

To get a more concrete idea of what this means, it may be well to list some characteristics of good liturgy. First, some theological considerations: good liturgy is liturgy that is

- response to God's call;
- surrender to God's transforming action;
- critique of our daily Christian living;
- expression of the whole Body of Christ;
- symbolic of our pilgrimage to eternal glory;
- enactment of the dynamic of the paschal mystery;
- embrace of the action of the Holy Spirit;
- encounter with divine presence.

Second, some practical considerations: good liturgy is liturgy that is

- choreographed toward graceful ritual;
- celebrated in aesthetically pleasing and appropriate sacred space;
- served by prepared, committed members of the assembly;
- properly paced, with space for silence;
- reflective of the liturgical season or feast;
- respectful of daily, weekly, seasonal rhythms;
- focused on rich symbolic action;
- uncluttered by anything that draws us away from the central action;
- inclusive of all members of the Body of Christ;
- musically rich with fitting balance;
- filled with joyful sounds, delightful tastes, uplifting smells, fluid movement, warm touch, challenging sights.

These considerations are an ideal or measure; each liturgical community needs to reflect carefully on them, and then qualify or add items that are pertinent to a particular situation. The important point is that good liturgy demands ongoing reflection, evaluation, and constant adjustments. Rather than a daunting task, working toward an ever more fruitful celebration of liturgy is an exciting counterpart to working toward an ever more faithful living of Christianity.

Authentic Liturgical Spirituality

Just as good liturgy may seem abstract and elusive until we break it down into manageable pieces upon which we can reflect and evaluate, so the same is true about authentic liturgical spirituality. This is to say that liturgical spirituality isn't just how one happens to be living the Gospel, but it also has certain criteria against which we might constantly measure our daily living. Again, we list some theological and practical considerations.

First, some theological considerations: an authentic liturgical spirituality

- flows from the dynamic dying and rising of liturgical action;
- is grounded in Sacred Scripture;
- is a surrender to the transforming Spirit within;
- thrusts us toward ecclesial integrity;
- is a reminder of God's ever-faithful, saving presence;
- prompts us toward embracing Jesus' mission to live for others;
- is a belief in and living out of our common identity as the Body of Christ;
- encourages us to Gospel living.

Second, some practical considerations: an authentic liturgical spirituality

- has daily ups and downs that are experienced as the rhythm of the paschal mystery;
- compels us to reach out to others in need as a recognition of the other as the Body of Christ;
- sees all aspects of life as ministry, as expressions of who we are as the Body of Christ;
- perceives and treats all life and creation as sacred;
- motivates us to do good as our response to God's unfailing action on our behalf;
- encourages us to make everyday choices to do God's will, which are an extension of our surrender during liturgy.

Again, these latter two lists are not intended to be exhaustive and should be critiqued and amended by each liturgical community and individual members.

There are obvious parallels between the lists, and this suggests that there are parallels between what we do in liturgy and what we do in our everyday Gospel living. Herein lies the import of liturgical spirituality: our everyday living parallels (reflects, mirrors, images) what liturgy is all about– entering into the dying/rising mystery of Christ, such that we are transformed ever more perfectly into being the Body of Christ. Liturgical spirituality is a concrete expression of our embracing the life and ministry of Jesus. It is challenging and demanding. It is death dealing and life giving. It is our being the risen Christ for others.

Paschal Mystery Revisited

The paschal mystery is a concept with which we are all more or less familiar. We know it has to do with the dying and rising mystery of Christ. We know that through baptism we are plunged into this mystery (see Rom 6, as we discussed in chap. 1), and so in some way we too are to embrace and live the paschal mystery. But for all too many of us, this is as far as it goes. To move paschal mystery beyond a theological concept to a reality to be lived—to move paschal mystery to what lies at the root of a spirituality of the assembly—is another matter, indeed, and a challenge.

Dying to self, self-sacrificing, self-giving, self-emptying, surrender, unbounded concern for others, poverty of self are all part of paschal mystery living. For many of us, however, this leads more to a discipline (as good as that may well be) rather than a joyful way of living. We forget that this is only one part of the paschal mystery, which is a dynamic rhythm of dying and rising, self-emptying and exaltation, poverty of self and fullness of risen life. Always, on this side of heaven, there will be both dying and rising. For paschal mystery to be a joyful way of living, we must live beyond its demands on self to where that self-giving leads: to new life.

Here is the crux of the mystery: in the very dying is the rising, in the very self-emptying is the exaltation, in the very poverty is found fullness. What this means is that in the dying, the self-emptying, the poverty is already new life. The reason for this bold statement is that by our self-giving, by our surrendering our wills to do God's will, by our choosing to make doing good for others a centerpiece of our life, we are most conforming ourselves to Christ. Only in this conformity—becoming ever more perfect members of the Body of Christ—can we say that we are growing in our identity with Christ, our identity as the Body of Christ, our identity as liturgical assembly, our identity as his disciples, our identity as Christians. Paschal mystery living, then, is about being who we are—members of Christ's Body. It means that we strive to model our lives ever more perfectly on Gospel values. In this kind of daily living is our holiness, our becoming evermore the images of the God who creates.

Rather than merely a negative choice, self-emptying is positive in its thrust. For Christ, emptying himself of divinity (see Phil 2:5-11) opened the way for him to become fully human, to be one with us in all things except sin. He even had to embrace human death. For us, emptying ourselves of whatever in us is not of the image of God makes room for us to embrace the indwelling of the Spirit, makes room for us to receive the abundance of divine life God offers us as a freely given gift. Notice here the presence of the Trinity. This understanding of the paschal mystery helps us see the three divine Persons all bound up with our self-emptying: the Son models for us self-emptying by becoming human and thus invites our own self-emptying; the Spirit dwells within us as the life-gift of the Father. Notice too that it is impossible to speak of self-emptying in this way without also speaking of our exaltation, the glory we receive by being given the very life of God. As we open ourselves to God, embrace the Spirit's indwelling, we are graced in such a way as to participate in divine life. A trinitarian understanding of the paschal mystery enables us to move beyond a focus only on Christ and his mystery to seeing the whole mystery of salvation as a trinitarian event by which we come to wholeness and fullness. This also makes clear the eschatological (referring to final glory at the end of times) thrust of our Christian living—we die and live ourselves into eternity; we empty and God fills ourselves into eternity; our living of the paschal mystery is a groaning toward the fullness of life that is promised. Poverty of self is not measured by what we have or don't have; it is measured by our willingness to empty ourselves for the sake of others. In the poverty, in the self-emptying, God fills us with more than we could ever earn, ever imagine, ever ask. God fills us with divine life.

This has enormous ramifications for how we celebrate liturgy and how we live. Liturgy enacts the paschal mystery; therefore, our participation in liturgy enacts our self-emptying and exaltation, our poverty of self and fullness of life. What we do in liturgy is a ritualization of what our whole Christian living is to be. The self-emptying and exaltation rhythm of liturgy is to be carried forward into the way we live every day. Since the rhythm of the paschal mystery is relational at root, then all of our encounters with others are part of this great mystery of God's desire to share divine life with us, to raise us up to be partakers of divinity.

Rhythm of Liturgy and Life, Self and Seasons

Our reflection on good liturgy and the paschal mystery brings us to an important conclusion: what we do at liturgy (make present the paschal mystery by embracing self-emptying and exaltation in the ritual itself) is exactly how we are to live every day. Faithful Gospel living in itself is a kind of "liturgy" of and for the world. The spirituality of the liturgical assembly is living this "liturgy" every day. It is self-emptying for the sake of others. It is a defining rhythm of life.

Each day unfolds as a rhythm between sunup and sundown. When the sun rises, there is light. Morning is an appropriate time to celebrate the resurrection: as the sun rises, we celebrate the Son's rising. Evening, on the other hand, when the sun sinks in the sky, sets, dies, there is darkness. We celebrate the dying of the Son. Evening is an appropriate time to reflect on the dark emptiness of saying no to God's will, to thank God for the graces of the day, to remember those who have died.

At one time in the church it was customary for Christians to assemble to pray at morning and evening in such a way as to remember that our days are marked by the sun and the Son's rhythm of rising and dying. Eventually this daily, common prayer of the church became the prayer of the clergy and monastics. The faithful laity were left to their own devotions for morning and evening prayer. Many of us grew up with the morning offering as our morning prayer and the guardian angel prayer before we went to bed. But these prayers, as wonderful and dear as they are, did not draw us into the paschal mystery rhythm. Recently, and happily, the daily missalette resources are including a simple Morning and Evening Prayer, consisting of psalm and intercessions that give us an opportunity to recapture the early church's practice of liturgical Morning and Evening Prayer. The importance of this prayer is that it thrusts us into the paschal mystery rhythm; it thrusts us into the saving mystery of Christ day in and day out.

In addition to the daily rhythm of paschal mystery in our prayer, the church also gives us a weekly rhythm of self-emptying and exaltation. The rhythm is played out between weekdays and Sundays. Monday through Saturday we work as if everything depends upon us. We care for our families, for others in need, for the natural resources of this good earth that have been given into our care. We work hard. Each day has its own dying to self, its own self-emptying, its own poverty of self. Each day has its own demands. Life would not be so bearable if all our daily demands did not open up on a wonderful day of resurrection. Each Sunday is celebrated to remember Christ's rising, his conquering sin and death.

In the early church, when Christians were freed by Constantine's Edict of Milan to practice their religion openly, their numbers grew so that erecting larger buildings to gather for liturgy became necessary. When possible they would build on top of a martyr's tomb. Martyrs have always been especially venerated in the church because they conformed their lives to Christ's, even to the point of physically dying for Christ and rising into eternal glory with him. Assembling for liturgy at their places of burial made a strong connection between the celebration of Mass and the resurrection. This is why the church chooses Sunday as the primary day for celebration of Mass: it is a celebration of Christ's Easter victory. This is why Sunday is a day of joy. This is why Sunday is a day of rest. Six days a week we work; on Sunday we rest from our productive work as a reminder that all we are and all we have is a gift of God. The Sunday rest is a reminder that we are ultimately totally dependent upon God. The weekly rhythm of the paschal mystery plays out between weekdays and Sundays, between work and rest. We need Sunday Mass to be nourished by the risen Christ's continual self-giving. Without this nourishment from the Bread of Life and Chalice of Salvation, we quickly lose sight of our baptismal commitment to Gospel living. Christ's self-giving at Mass on the altar is our self-giving on the altar of the world.

We have briefly reflected on the daily and weekly rhythm of the paschal mystery, a rhythm that defines our Gospel living and is expressed as a liturgical spirituality. There is a proper liturgy for each day (Morning and Evening Prayer) and for each week (Mass, the celebration of Eucharist). We turn now to a third rhythm that marks a liturgical spirituality. This rhythm is the yearly rhythm of liturgical seasons. No specific liturgy expresses the rhythm of the liturgical year. Instead, where we are in the liturgical year colors how we celebrate our daily and weekly liturgies.

At one time the liturgical year began at the Easter Vigil. As the liturgical year developed, with more festivals being added, the beginning of the liturgical year became the First Sunday of Advent. With a more historical mentality, the sense was that we begin at the beginning of Jesus' life, at the incarnation. Our present understanding of the liturgical year sets aside a historical mentality and reflects on the liturgical year as unfolding the whole of Jesus' saving mystery. Let us briefly reflect on how each liturgical season makes present the rhythm of the paschal mystery and, therefore, draws us deeper into a liturgical spirituality.

Advent

Advent is a season of four Sundays, not of four weeks. The length of Advent depends upon what day of the week Christmas falls. The longest Advent season happens when Christmas is on Sunday; the shortest Advent is when Christmas is on Monday and Christmas Eve and the Fourth Sunday of Advent coincide.

Advent is a time to celebrate the comings of Christ. The temptation is to focus on Christmas from the very beginning; the Lectionary actually prompts us to focus on the second coming of Christ at the end of time during the first two weeks of Advent; only with the Third Sunday of Advent do we liturgically turn to focusing on the birth of Christ (this is why Advent must be a season of four Sundays, so the Sundays are evenly divided between the second and first comings of Christ). Therefore, Advent is a single season pointing to two comings of Christ—at the end of time in final glory and at his human birth at the beginning of the Christian era.

The first part of Advent, then, would include expecting judgment (in this context penance during Advent is appropriate) and Christ's promise to return to gather all into his glory, celebrating Christ's victory and reign, and being prepared for the many comings of Christ into our lives. Here, we clearly see a paschal mystery rhythm. The second part of Advent focuses on the mystery of the incarnation proper, but the emphasis is more on our Savior's *coming* than on the birth of a baby many centuries ago. The celebration of the incarnation is surely one of great joy. But the three days right after Christmas are feasts reminding us of the cost of this joy. The feasts of St. Stephen the First Martyr (December 26), St. John the Evangelist (December 27), and the Holy Innocents (December 28) all remind us of the self-emptying that living Christ's saving mystery demands.

Christmas/Epiphany

Christmas celebrates salvation rather than a birthday. Yes, we commemorate the birth of the infant and all the miraculous divine interventions and human cooperation that brought it about. The overall import of the season, however, is that this Child is named "Jesus"—Savior. The birth is for our sake and for our salvation. This is the focus of our festivity: God's graciousness and mercy in choosing to be present to us in a human form. In the incarnation divinity is wedded to humanity and we are given the opportunity to choose to be raised up to share in that same divine life. Our share in this life is a matter of our emptying ourselves of all that gets in the way of growing in our graced relationship with God. Again, the rhythm of dying and rising.

Light, glory, joy, peace are words that are frequently spoken in the Scripture proclamations throughout this festal season. Moreover, the movement in the season itself—from birth (Christmas) to manifestation to Gentiles (epiphany) to public ministry (Jesus' baptism)—draws us into the mystery of why Jesus came: so that all peoples might share in the glory of his eternal life.

It is fitting that the Christmas/Epiphany season concludes with a celebration of the baptism of Jesus, which is also the First Sunday in Ordinary Time. Baptism (as we saw in chap. 1) draws us into the saving mystery of Jesus, the very reason for the incarnation. Christmas and Epiphany are essentially festivals of salvation. Baptism is a festival calling us to live what we have just celebrated: Emmanuel, God is with us. Now in us and through us.

Ordinary Time

It is sometimes difficult to keep in mind that Ordinary Time is a single season because it is divided into two parts—the first part linking Advent/Christmas/Epiphany with Lent/Triduum/ Easter and the second part linking Lent/Triduum/Easter with Advent/Christmas/Epiphany. In a real sense, then, Ordinary Time helps us bridge the two festal seasons and link them together. Thus, there is a paschal mystery rhythm between the festal seasons (which celebrate the victory of Christ over sin and death) and Ordinary Time (which calls us to Gospel living).

Throughout the year we commemorate the one paschal mystery of Christ in which we participate by our baptism, and so the two festal seasons are really two sides of the same saving act and Ordinary Time is our Gospel journey connecting the differing expressions of Christ's saving act. The primary characteristic of Ordinary Time is that we read successively at Sunday Mass from one of the Synoptic Gospels (Matthew during Year A, Mark during Year B, and Luke during Year C). All the Synoptic Gospels share a structure that begins with Jesus' birth (Matthew and Luke) or public ministry (Mark) and ends in Jerusalem with the death and resurrection (albeit each gospel develops this journey to Jerusalem in quite different ways).

During Ordinary Time we walk with Jesus through his public ministry to Jerusalem, to his dying and rising. Thus Ordinary Time is our "paschal mystery" journey. How well we celebrate Ordinary Time affects how well we are able to enter the depths of the festal seasons. Ordinary Time is the longest liturgical season. It is as though the church knows that we need a long period of time to hear the demands of the Gospel. Ordinary Time is the church's teaching time. By walking with Jesus toward Jerusalem, we experience all the disappointments and demands, the frustrations and failures, the successes and prayer that following him requires. Ordinary Time is the "dying" season of the church's year, but within the dying we experience the risings, the life God constantly offers us when we choose to be faithful followers.

Lent

At first glance, we might think of Lent as primarily a season of sacrifice, of giving up, of living through it as best we can; the good thing about Lent is that it will be over. While penance certainly is part of Lent, our penance is not for its own sake. Its purpose is to bring us to conversion, to a greater commitment to Gospel living. Lent is the time when those preparing for baptism at the Easter Vigil make their final preparations. We join with them in their journey to baptism as we prepare to renew our own baptismal promises at Easter.

Lent is a period of forty fast days (the season is actually longer than forty days because Sundays are never fast days, even during Lent) that call us to conversion of life and renewed seriousness about our faithful discipleship. Lent is a season marked by penance, which traditionally includes three practices—prayer, fasting, and almsgiving (charity). Lent is a sober season, but not a somber one. Our penance is practice in the self-emptying and poverty of self that is part of the paschal mystery rhythm. Lent is a time when our penance brings home most clearly how we must die with Christ if we are to rise with him.

A good preparation during Lent opens up a deeper possibility for a fuller celebration at Easter. The penitential discipline of Lent is a time for us to renew our dying to self—we spend ourselves in self-sacrifice for others. Only by this dying to self can the new life of Easter truly take us by surprise and open us in new ways to the wonders God offers us.

Sacred Triduum

The Sacred Triduum (a word meaning "three days") is the most sacred three days of the entire liturgical year. It begins with the celebration of the Mass of the Lord's Supper on Holy

Thursday evening and concludes with evening prayer on Easter Sunday (see Universal Norms on the Liturgical Year and the General Roman Calendar). This is the day (the three days really are celebrated as one day) when we commemorate in a most solemn way Christ's paschal sacrifice—his surrendering to death, lying in the tomb, and rising on the third day. This is the day when everything of the entire liturgical year rises to a climax, when we celebrate in a most profound way God's gift of salvation.

The Triduum as three days might appear confusing because we celebrate it on Holy Thursday, Good Friday, Holy Saturday, and Easter Sunday—that's four days. However, on major festivals during the liturgical year, as well as on each Sunday, the church changes how we count a day. Most of the time, our days are counted from midnight to midnight; this is the time frame of our workdays. On Sundays and big feast days the church returns to the Jewish reckoning of day, which is from sundown until sundown. So, the Triduum is three days: from sundown on Holy Thursday through sundown on Easter Sunday.

Each day has its special meaning at the same time that the Triduum is a unified celebration of one mystery. Holy Thursday is celebrated in an evening of quiet joy that remembers Jesus' giving us his very Body and Blood as our nourishment, Jesus' giving us a model for serving others, and the day when we celebrate the unity of ordained priests with their bishop. In this celebration, we remember—we make present—the grace-gift of Jesus' Body and Blood as well as the call to serve others. Rising and dying. Exaltation and self-emptying. Poverty of self and fullness of life.

Good Friday is the most sober day of the year, but it is not a sad day. It is a day on which there is quiet joy because this day Jesus willingly went to his death out of love for us, as we so solemnly proclaim in John's passion account and pray for the needs of the world in the solemn prayers. In John's passion, always proclaimed on Good Friday, Jesus is in charge. A dozen times in the account the word "king" appears. Jesus is sovereign. Death is not imposed upon him by some human trial and judgment.

He accepts death because this is where unwavering fidelity to his Father's will leads. By accepting death, Jesus is triumphant. The world is redeemed. Yet, there is much saving work to be done, as is evidenced in our praying the solemn prayers of intercession. Rising and dying. Exaltation and self-emptying. Poverty of self and fullness of life.

Holy Saturday is a day of preparation for the greatest of all vigils celebrated in the night of Holy Saturday. At the Easter Vigil we bless and light the new fire and light and process with the Easter candle because Christ our Light has conquered the darkness of sin and death; we ponder during an extended proclamation of Scripture God's mighty deeds of salvation; we sing our first Easter alleluias and hear once more the Easter gospel's proclamation that Jesus has risen; we initiate and welcome new members; we are sent forth to live the Easter mystery with alleluias ringing in our ears. Perhaps of all the liturgies we celebrate in a given year, this one illustrates most clearly the rhythm of dying and rising: darkness and light, sin and redemption, death and life. Dying and rising. Self-emptying and exaltation. Poverty of self and fullness of life.

Easter

Easter is a one-day celebration (the Easter Vigil and Easter Sunday); an eight-day celebration (the octave of Easter, with each day of Easter week being celebrated as a solemnity); and a great octave, a fifty-day celebration (only concluding with Evening Prayer on Pentecost). These are the fifty days during which we try to comprehend more deeply that Christ is risen and desires to share that risen life with us; that Jesus is the Good Shepherd who cares for us and never abandons us; that Jesus calls us to be faithful disciples, prays for us, teaches us, and promises the Holy Spirit will be with us to bring us peace and guide us in our task of discipleship.

Each day of the fifty days draws us to Pentecost when we celebrate the gift of the Spirit who dwells within each of us. On the Fifth, Sixth, and Seventh Sundays of Easter (for most dioceses in the United States the Seventh Sunday drops out and is replaced with the celebration of the Ascension) the gospels are taken from Jesus' great prayer at the Last Supper for his disciples. He knows his ministry of salvation is being passed on to them. They will continue his sacred work. But this is no easy task. Like Jesus, his followers will be rejected, ridiculed, challenged, tried, condemned. Jesus is quite compassionate in praying for his disciples. He knows that our disciple life will be no easier than was his ministry. But with his prayer and constant companionship, we have all we need to remain faithful. We have all we need to come to the same risen glory to which his Father raised him. Easter is a fifty-day celebration of unbounded joy in risen life, quiet confidence that we already share in that life, and courageous acceptance of taking up our own task to be Jesus' disciples. Dying and rising. Self-emptying and exaltation. Poverty of self and fullness of life.

The rhythm of the liturgical year is self-defining. When we enter daily, weekly, yearly into the rhythm of self-emptying and exaltation, we are living the spirituality that brings the fullness of life. The ministry of the assembly is ultimately to enter into this way of living that brings us home to eternal life with God.

Liturgical colors. Each season of the liturgical year as well as each festival we celebrate has a special color assigned to it. They were not arbitrarily chosen but have specific, symbolic meaning. Eventually various colors became part of liturgical celebrations around the end of the first millennium; when vestments and other accoutrements were normalized, it was natural to normalize colors too. The colors haven't always been the six we presently are permitted to use (violet, white, green, red, rose, black), but these have become standard because they convey certain meanings about the seasons and days with which they are associated.

Violet. The US national *ordo* (list of festivals and seasons with information on various liturgical elements, such as the Lectionary readings) indicates violet is the color for both Advent and Lent. A problem occurs when we try to interpret the color "violet." If we look to the Latin, it gets even more confusing because *purpura* refers to the crayfish from which in ancient times purple dye was extracted. This was a costly process and only royalty and the very rich could afford things dyed this color. Hence, we use the language "royal purple" as one way to designate this color. Royal purple is a blue purple. Red and blue dyes or pigments mixed together make purple; blue purple has more blue than red dye or pigment. Since Advent begins with an eschatological (referring to final fulfillment at the end of times) motif and begins on the Sunday after we celebrate the Solemnity of Our Lord Jesus Christ, King of the Universe, this "royal" or blue purple would be a good choice for this season. Since the United States bishops have not approved blue as a liturgical color, it is not used during Advent (nor for Marian festivals). The violet for Lent might appropriately be a red purple, which conveys more of a penitential sense marking this season; muted colors can also be effective for conveying the soberness of the Lenten season.

White/gold/silver. In our Western culture white is a color symbolizing purity, integrity of life, and festivity. Liturgically, white is used on most of the high festivals (Pentecost is a notable exception), festival days of saints who are not martyrs, and festivals honoring the Blessed Virgin Mary. It has also been traditional (and is permitted in the United States) to adorn white vestments with gold and silver embroidery or even to use gold and silver vestments on the most solemn festivals such as Christmas and Easter.

Green. Green is nature's most abundant color and speaks to us of life. It is the color for Ordinary Time. Green conveys to us the lushness of nature and the bursting forth of new life. Ordinary Time is that time of the liturgical year characterized by a semi-continuous reading of one of the Synoptic Gospels (Matthew, Mark, or Luke)—the time when we walk with Jesus through his public ministry toward Jerusalem and dying but also toward the new life of the resurrection. Green is also a color of hope—our faithful discipleship will bring us to eternal life.

Red. Red is the color of blood and is used for festivals of martyrs and apostles (because they were martyrs; white, however, is used for St. John on December 27), on Palm Sunday, and on Good Friday where it symbolizes the willing self-sacrifice of one's life for salvation. Red is also worn on Pentecost to symbolize the tongues of fire whereby the Holy Spirit descended upon the apostles. Red is an intense color used on feast days that speak to us ever so strongly of the cost of our faith and the gift of our faith.

Rose. In the United States rose may still be worn where it has been the custom, but in most parishes it has fallen into disuse. This color may be worn on only two Sundays of the year: on *Gaudete* Sunday (the Third Sunday of Advent) and on *Laetare* Sunday (the Fourth Sunday of Lent). Worn halfway through these two seasons, rose symbolizes the anticipated end of our period of penance and the joyful beginning of our celebrations of Christmas and Easter. We now have a different understanding of the meaning of these two seasons: Advent's penance is related to the judgment at Christ's second coming and Lent's penance is related to conversion of life and the final preparation for baptism by the elect or the renewal of our baptismal promises by the faithful. Hence, the use of rose vestments halfway through these seasons in a sense of "almost there, we can make it" is probably not very meaningful.

Black. Black (and violet) is permitted in the United States for funerals and Masses for the Dead, but white is almost always chosen for these occasions because of a renewed understanding of death as the doorway to the new life of the resurrection.

Hospitality of Self

The word "hospitality" is derived from the Latin *hospes*, meaning "stranger, guest." We have a number of English words with roots in this Latin: hospital, hotel, hostel, hospice. Hospitality has to do with "at-homeness." Elisha the prophet developed a habit of accepting the hospitality of a wealthy woman whenever he passed along her way. Convinced that Elisha was "a holy man of God," the woman said to her husband, "Let us make a small roof chamber with walls, and put there for him a bed, a table, a chair, and a lamp, so that he can stay there whenever he comes to us" (2 Kgs 4:9-10). This woman not only opened her home to Elisha, she made for him a home, a place of his own where he could find rest and solitude.

This marvelous example of hospitality suggests to us that opening ourselves to receive another is far more than merely providing the necessities of life. Israel's practice of hospitality by caring for the stranger was motivated by God's actions. God was hospitable to Israel by calling them out of slavery, caring for them in the desert, giving them a homeland overflowing with milk and honey. So whenever Israel practiced hospitality, it was a way of remembering God's gracious deeds toward them.

Liturgical hospitality must be a matter of making the stranger a guest at home. We might even argue that at liturgy there can be no stranger, because through baptism we are all made members of the one Body of Christ. Even when there are those among us who are not baptized Christians, our welcome reaches out to them because all believers are members of the household of God. Each member of the liturgical assembly, as an act of hospitality and expression of ministry, willingly welcomes all into our midst. We might turn this notion of liturgical hospitality around too. In liturgy we are all strangers whom Christ as host invites into his family as guests, forgiving all that alienates us and welcoming us, such that we are transformed from strangers into being richer members at home in the Body of Christ.

The hospitality that is part and parcel of liturgy can be measured rather easily. Our hospitality is marked not only by the smiles and concern we show each other as we gather for liturgy; not only by remembering all the church, the needs of the world, the poor and sick and others in need at the universal prayer (prayer of the faithful); but also by the way we live liturgy by being hospitable to others beyond the church walls. Again, our ministry as assembly members spills out beyond the liturgical rite into the way we live. As Christ calls us home each liturgy to be one with him and nourishes us on his very Body and Blood, we call others "home" to us, to be an encounter for them of Christ. Welcoming each other to liturgy with friendly greetings is pointless and shallow if what we do together during liturgy doesn't make us more charitable, just, truthful, or act with more integrity beyond liturgy. Hospitality is not just for inside the church walls; it is also to be outside for all the world.

In all things we are to be hospitable, that is, receive anyone who comes, respond to any need, be Christ's presence in all circumstances. In a word, we are to be home for those who search for a home. There can be no stranger among us. There can be no welcoming that is too much trouble. There can be no demands on us that are received as an annoyance. Just as Christ embraces all in the wide arms of his compassion and care, so must we. Our liturgical spirituality calls us to the kind of self-giving, self-emptying, self-sacrificing that conveys a spirit of peace and dignity, goodness and wholeness to anyone who crosses the path of our life journey. Our spirituality opens our hearts as homes for anyone who comes. It bids us to touch the weak and needy, the strong and wealthy among us with an "at-homeness" that assures them of Christ's love and presence.

The wealthy woman who accommodated Elisha did more than simply receive him into her home. She anticipated his arrival, preparing a place of his own where he would be at home among "family." Our liturgical spirituality and our ministry as assembly call us to anticipate being home, being bread for others. We must offer kindness before it is needed, generosity before it is required, forgiveness before it is asked, healing before sickness even shows, patience before it is necessary. Being bread for others means that our very selves are the home where others encounter Christ. Eucharist is our true home. Liturgical spirituality brings us home. Again and again.

Conclusion

In the previous five chapters we have made many assertions about the ministry of the assembly. We have reflected on liturgical gestures and postures, spaces and symbols, objects and actions. All of this contributes to a rich, rich complex of words, actions, silences, singing, and movement that together make up a liturgical celebration. Our ministry as a liturgical assembly is to respond to God's summons to the divine presence, to surrender to the demands of the celebration, to unite ourselves with Christ's self-giving, to lift hearts to God in thankfulness and praise, to receive the transforming grace God offers us, to live every day what we celebrate. The ministry of the assembly is who we are and what we do at liturgy; it is who we are and what we do in our daily living.

The key to this ministry is that we are baptized into Jesus' death and resurrection. Baptism conforms us to Christ so closely that we are members of his very Body who are commissioned to continue his saving ministry every day, in our little corner of the world. We are temples of the Holy Spirit who, by God's life coursing within us, are presences of the risen Christ to all we meet. This ministry makes demands on us: it calls us to die to ourselves, to empty ourselves of all that weakens our bond in Christ, to be self-giving and self-sacrificing for the good of others. In this very surrender of ourselves, we conform ourselves more perfectly to Christ. As we grow into Christ, we grow into a deeper share in his exaltation, his glory, which we receive now but in its fullness in the eternal life to come.

We spell out in concrete terms the characteristics of the ministry of the assembly, who we are and whom we seek to become. The ministry of the assembly

- is the Body of Christ made visible in our world today;
- focuses on our common identity united under Jesus Christ, the Head;
- continues in our being and actions Jesus' saving mission;
- is imbued with other-centeredness;
- surrenders to God's transforming action within its members;
- accepts diversity with heartfelt hospitality;
- recognizes each member's place and role in diversity;
- has real commitment to celebrating liturgy well;
- balances liturgical and devotional prayer;
- surrenders to the dynamic flow of the rite;
- respects ritual moments/movements/demands;
- understands that Christian living flows to and from liturgy;
- lives the daily, weekly, and yearly rhythm of the paschal mystery that liturgy enacts.

None of these characteristics is such that we can "conquer" them and say we've finished our ministry as an assembly. They all take a lifetime of learning and commitment, of learning anew and recommitting ourselves to living as Jesus calls us. Jesus entrusts his saving mission to us. Holding this as a sacred trust, living the paschal mystery as best we can, reaching out to recognize the dignity we all share in Christ is what the ministry of the assembly is all about.

Will we be perfect ministers? Not on this side of heaven. Will we be good ministers? We certainly will, if we surrender ourselves to the transforming power of God unleashed during liturgy and live this each day. God is a saving, merciful, compassionate, forgiving, loving God. God sent the divine Son to become one with us. The Father and Son send their Holy Spirit to dwell within us. Such dignity, such grace, such love God shows us. The ministry of the assembly is to return this love with our whole hearts.

Notes

Introduction

1. The General Instruction of the Roman Missal, Congregation for Divine Worship and the Discipline of the Sacraments (ICEL, 2011), 91, italics added. Hereafter cited as GIRM.

2. *Sacrosanctum Concilium* (The Constitution on the Sacred Liturgy), 19, the first document passed by the council fathers, promulgated on December 4, 1963. Austin Flannery, ed., *Vatican Council II: Constitutions, Decrees, Declarations; The Basic Sixteen Documents* (Collegeville, MN: Liturgical Press, 2014). Hereafter cited as SC.

Chapter Two

1. A numbering system used in official documents of the Catholic Church; "paragraph" can actually include more than one grammatical paragraph.

Chapter Four

1. See also GIRM 122 and *Built of Living Stones: Art, Architecture, and Worship*, Guidelines of the National Conference of Catholic Bishops (Washington, DC: United States Catholic Conference, 2000), 91.